CLEAN SOUPS

CLEAN SOUPS

Simple, Nourishing Recipes for Health and Vitality

REBECCA KATZ

with Mat Edelson

photography by Eva Kolenko

TEN SPEED PRESS

Berkeley

for my soup sister,
julie fischer burford

introduction

I came by my love of soup-making honestly. It's in my blood. I spent many a childhood afternoon sitting with my feet dangling off the kitchen counter, watching in wonder as my mother and grandmother chopped and stirred, creating culinary wonders in a flame-enameled Le Creuset pot.

The soups they made were magic. I always felt better after having a cup or bowl, and I knew instinctively that soup had the power to heal. There was something about soup that enchanted me from the get-go. I think I instinctively knew that soup had the power to heal not only me, but others as well. When I was at Northwestern University, exhausted classmates would straggle by at all hours looking for a bowl of my nana's chicken soup (see page 96).

It wasn't until later that I met my soup mentor, chef Rich LaMarita of the Natural Gourmet Institute for Health and Culinary Arts. Rich is a larger-than-life character who looks like he came right out of central casting. The first time I saw him, he was lecturing while standing over a twenty-three-quart stockpot of simmering fennel stock. Every few minutes he would pause, remove the lid, and wave his hand over the pot to waft the steam toward his nose. He'd inhale deeply, nod approvingly, then replace the lid. Rich was all about using all your senses to navigate a soup to fruition. His appearance and knowledge left me a bit awestruck (and a little intimidated) at first, but when we finally had a chance to work together, his jovial smile quickly reassured me. He saw that I wasn't a novice at soup-making—I had learned to constantly taste my soup while it was simmering, to course-correct. He pulled me aside one day and said, "You have the instincts to become a master soup-maker. I'm going to teach you everything I know about soups!"

And he did. Throughout my twenty-year culinary consulting and cooking career in the food-as-medicine movement, I've been, first and foremost, a soup-maker. I've practiced my craft in kitchens as diverse as the Chopra Center for Wellbeing, Dr. Andrew Weil's Arizona Center for Integrative Medicine's annual Nutrition and Health Conference, and the Commonweal Retreat Center in Bolinas, California. It was at Commonweal's retreats, when I was often cooking for seriously ill people, that I realized how energizing a nutrient-dense, delicious soup could be. It was amazing: people who could barely eat would return again and again to the soup pot. I was doling out a little liquid health with each dip of the ladle.

I guess that makes me just the latest in a very long line of soup shamans. Some people may think of soup-making for health purposes as a trend. But the truth is, from the Baha'i to the Buddhists, and from the Christians to the simply curious, using soup to help the body detoxify and renew itself is as old as humankind. Hippocrates and Greek physicians used bone broths as a curative for the sick and fatigued.

Flash forward a couple of millenia, and you've got companies coming out of the woodwork promoting their healthy soups. Sure, if you want to spend up to $300 for a week's worth of commercially made soups, this is a possible option, but wouldn't you rather learn from a master how to make healthy soups on your own? Delicious soups that you can pull together in a half hour or less can lead you to true soup empowerment.

It's really that easy, as you'll see in this book. And it's really that healthy. Eating soup is a way to hit the body's reset button, to allow internal organs devoted to detoxification the rest and nutrients necessary to successfully do their job. The result, from a health viewpoint, is often startling, but no one should really be surprised. Soup, after all, is life distilled into a bowl. Unlike juicing, nothing is lost in the stockpot; indeed, just the opposite takes place. The heat of the pot slowly breaks down nutrients to a more digestible state, simultaneously releasing outrageous flavors that create heady aromas that magnetically draw us to the broth.

This book is dedicated to the proposition that everyone can enjoy making soup, whether the goal is a full-blown, two-day, nothing-but-soup cleanse, or a more general commitment to incorporate soup on a daily or weekly basis. Believe me, the ability to create culinary alchemy in a pot can be learned (I'm living proof), and the payoff is so high: when you're feeling out of sorts, and your appetite or digestion may be off, soup is the absolutely best way to make a healthy reconnection with food. It's like taking your body to a spa. You'll come out feeling marvelous.

the soup tool kit

Learning to be a great soup-maker isn't a mystery; it's all about tactically approaching your goal, be it a weekend cleanse or just a general desire to get more soup into your life. What you need for soup success is a plan that minimizes stress and maximizes your pleasure in the kitchen.

That's where this chapter comes in. I start with the basics, including a complete list of the equipment you'll need (my mantra: always have the right tool for the job). I'll also show you how to stock your pantry, which is a huge time-saver. When you realize that three-quarters of what you need to make a given soup is already in your pantry, your enthusiasm to cook will skyrocket exponentially.

Similarly, having broths at your command is foundational to turning out numerous delicious soups quickly and efficiently. I've come up with a diagram (see page 33) that explains how you can take one basic eight-quart pot of broth and create two quarts each of four distinct new broths in just a few simple steps. These four new broths can easily be frozen and stored (see "Storage," page 12), ready to be turned into dozens of soups in a matter of minutes.

I'll also show you how all of the soups in this book follow a template (see page 20)—the dance steps, if you will, that each soup tangos to as it wends its way from water to wonderment. Once you pick up the moves—and believe me, they're easier than you think—you'll be on your way to being a master soup-maker in no time.

Understanding the template is the key to learning what I call "culinary improvisation." It's that ability that all good cooks have to substitute ingredients to suit the moment and mood. Initially, you might be concerned about riffing on a recipe, fearful that you'll wander into a never-never land where taste might suffer. Au contraire! I'll show you a foolproof way of course-correcting any soup using just four basic pantry staples. It's called FASS—fat, acid, salt, and sweet (see page 22)—and I absolutely guarantee that it will maximize the flavor of any soup you make.

pantry

Having the staples in the following table on hand allows cooking to be easy and creative. You don't have to go out and buy all of the ingredients listed at once. As you make your way through this book, your pantry will naturally expand as you shop and cook more often.

pantry 101

spices	oils	herbs and produce	dry and canned goods	flavor boosters
black pepper	coconut oil	basil	canned or dried cannellini beans	apple cider vinegar
curry powder	extra-virgin olive oil	carrots	canned or dried chickpeas	fish sauce
ground coriander and coriander seeds	ghee	celery	canned tomatoes	maple syrup
ground cumin		cilantro	coconut milk	miso
ground and fresh turmeric		flat-leaf parsley	french lentils	rice vinegar
red pepper flakes		garlic	raw cashews	tamari
saffron threads		ginger	shelled pistachios	tomato paste
sea salt		leeks		
		lemons		
		limes		
		mint		
		onions		
		sweet potatoes		

equipment

You can get by nicely without every piece I've listed here, but these are what I consider my essentials. They make my life easier in the kitchen, and they'll do the same for you. Refer to the resource guide on page 139 for sourcing.

POTS

* four- or six-quart heavy-bottomed pot with lid (enameled cast-iron or stainless steel); use for all standard soup recipes unless otherwise noted
* large skillet
* rimmed baking pans
* twelve-quart stockpot with lid

SMALL APPLIANCES

* blender (high-speed brand like Vitamix preferable)
* food processor
* immersion blender
* pressure cooker
* slow cooker (eight-quart or larger)

KITCHEN TOOLS

* cheesecloth
* citrus juicer
* cutting board
* knife
* ladle
* large bowl or container (to strain stock into)
* large colander or strainer
* microplane zester
* mixing bowls
* parchment paper
* spatula
* spiralizer or julienne peeler
* wooden spoon

storage

Broth is liquid gold. It's precious and should be stored in a way that preserves its taste and nutrition. Good labeling is important, because no one wants mystery food in the freezer. Choosing the right storage containers and knowing how to thaw and reheat is also key to getting the most mileage out of your creations (this includes not just broth, but also most soups and some toppers).

LABELING

Using painter's tape or masking tape, label your broth or soup with its name and the date you made it.

USE-BY DATE

For soups and broths, store for up to five days in the fridge, except for the fish soups (see pages 98 and 116), which can be stored up to three days.

For soups, store for up to three months in the freezer, and for broths, freeze up to six months.

CONTAINERS

If using glass containers be sure they're made of tempered glass that can be frozen. If you're using any type of plastic, be sure it's BPA-free and that the soup has cooled before storing. For to-go containers, the jars listed below are great options that I use regularly. If you want to keep your soup hot, get a thermos or other insulated container.

* Weck jars
* Ball jars (now available in tempered glass)
* Snapware or similar glass storage containers
* Ziplock bags
* BPA-free plastic containers
* To-go soup containers (usually lined with cardboard)

storing tips

* Freeze broth in usable portions—six cups for most broths, but two- and four-cup quantities will also be useful.

* Pack soup in 1½- to 2-cup serving sizes so it's ready to grab from the fridge or freezer.

* Prep veggies (fresh or roasted) and refrigerate them in airtight containers for up to four days.

* Strip kale from its stems and rip it into small pieces. Refrigerate it in an airtight container or baggie for up to four days.

* Crispy baked toppers should be stored in an airtight container at room temperature for up to five days.

* Dollops (pestos and nut creams) should be stored in an airtight container in the refrigerator for up to seven days or in the freezer for up to two months. Salsas can be stored for up to five days in the refrigerator.

Magic Mineral Broth

THAWING

You can thaw frozen soups in several ways:

- Place the container of soup in the fridge for two days before you want to use it. It will thaw in a day or two, depending on the size and shape of the storage container.
- Immerse the container in warm water to loosen the frozen soup from the sides. Then pop it out directly into a pot and let it thaw over medium-low heat, stirring to keep the soup from scalding.
- Place the soup in its container in a warm water bath until it is fully thawed.

Avoid thawing in the microwave, especially when the soup is in a plastic container. When plastic is heated, it can potentially leach chemicals into your food.

Be careful when freezing and thawing in glass jars. Make sure the glass is tempered and can handle the extreme temperature changes. When soup is frozen in glass jars, it doesn't pop out as easily as it does from plastic containers.

REHEATING

Many soups absorb most of the liquid when stored, resulting in a thick, paste-like consistency. Simply add ½ cup of broth or water, taste, and add a spritz of lemon juice, pinch of salt, or even fresh herbs if needed. Give it the spa treatment! Toppers (see page 119) are also great to give new life to reheated soups.

weekend jump-start cleanse

The cleanse outlined in this section isn't an unbendable prescription so much as a detailed suggestion for incorporating more soup into your life. A cleanse is all about rebooting your digestive tract and giving your body a chance to detox and feel good; this will occur (really!) whether you spend a weekend dedicated to the task or just opt to have soup on a more frequent basis.

If you're going to try a two-day cleanse, my advice is to do it over a weekend or whenever you have two days off from work. You need to see how your body reacts to a cleanse, and the best place to do that is at home, without the added stress of the workplace. Don't be surprised if a cleanse, by giving your digestion a break, leaves you feeling revitalized, rejuvenated, and energized. The only caveat I'd add is that if you feel a little light-headed on a cleanse, that's a sign that you haven't eaten enough. The solution? Have a little more soup. Remember, this isn't about starvation, but rather satiation.

The schedule on page 18 is a guideline to how you can mix and match soups to use for a cleanse. These are *only* suggestions. Once you get the hang of it, feel free to substitute any of the soups in the book that you enjoy in place of those listed on pages 18 and 19. The idea is that, in getting ready for a cleanse, you'd prepare a certain amount of soup. Optimally, that would include one broth, two blended soups, and two traditional soups. Here's how you utilize them (and again, these are just suggestions; do what works for you): For a snack or light meal, go with the blended soups. For dinner, or if you desire something a bit heartier, try a traditional soup. The broth? That becomes your go-to tonic throughout the day. You can put it in a thermos and sip it like a tea every few hours (feel free to add a spritz of lemon juice and a pinch of sea salt). The broths are incredibly nutrient dense, so a little can go a long way. On another note, even a one-day cleanse often yields noticeable benefits, so if you have a day free, go for it!

* Starting your day with a glass of warm or hot water with a spritz of lemon juice will wake up your digestive system.

* Eat soup every two hours.

* Drink plenty of water and green or herbal tea or broth throughout the day.

* Eat two to three cups of soup at mealtimes. If at any point you feel hungry, have broth or more soup.

* Give your digestive system a twelve-hour break (from dinner until breakfast). You want your last meal to be three hours before you go to bed for better sleep.

* Adding a dash of tamari or fish sauce or a pinch of salt to warmed broth will enhance the flavors. Adding a sprig of fresh thyme or rosemary will wake up your senses and make your cleanse more enjoyable.

* Take time to relax and do some light stretching or exercise. You should be able to go through all of your normal routines without feeling at all light-headed.

SCHEDULE

PREBREAKFAST	lemon water	1 cup
BREAKFAST	blended soup	2 to 3 cups
SNACK	blended soup	1 cup
LUNCH	traditional soup	2 to 3 cups
SNACK	blended soup	1 cup
DINNER	traditional soup	2 to 3 cups

Follow the same plan on day two, swapping out the blended soups for the traditional soups if you wish to mix it up.

Here are some of my suggested soups for a weekend cleanse. The broths will serve to keep you nourished and hydrated, while the soups will promote detoxification and regulate your blood sugar.

broths and stocks

Magic Mineral Broth (page 35)

Thai Coconut Broth (page 36)

Chicken Magic Mineral Broth (page 38)

Old-Fashioned Chicken Stock (page 39)

Immune Broth (page 40)

Nourishing Bone Broth (page 41)

Pastured Beef Bone Broth (page 43)

blended soups

Springtime Asparagus and Leek Soup (page 49)

Power Green Soup (page 58)

Golden Beet and Fennel Soup (page 61)

Kale Soup with Coconut and Lime (page 66)

Summer Zucchini Soup with Basil (page 73)

PLANNING AND PREPARING FOR A REVITALIZING CLEANSE

A little planning and preparation will set you up for a smooth cleanse.
You don't want to spend the entire two days cooking, but instead
relaxing and rejuvenating. This plan is flexible, so don't feel like you
need to do everything exactly when I say.

One week prior:

* Choose the recipes.

* Make a shopping list for
  the broths.

* Shop for the broths.

* Make the broths and store
  in six- and four-cup portions
  (see page 12).

Two days prior:

* Shop for the soups.

* Look for common ingredients
  across recipes and prepare
  them all at once—for example,
  chop all the onions, carrots,
  and garlic you need for the
  soups. If you won't be making
  all the soups that day, store any
  unused vegetables in an airtight
  container in the fridge.

* Make all of the blended soups.

* Store soup in portions for your
  two-day cleanse and freeze any
  leftovers.

One day prior:

* Make sure vegetables are the
  center of your plate in all your
  meals.

* If you think time will be tight
  the day of the cleanse, make
  the traditional soups
  beforehand.

how to make any soup

In the "Common Elements" chart, opposite, I deconstruct soups and show just how easy they are to make. You don't even need a recipe! All soups tend to have common elements: fat, aromatics, dried herbs and spices, deglazing liquid, main ingredients, broth, and finishers. Once you recognize the role each ingredient plays in a soup, you're on your way to freeing up your creativity, and you'll soon see a recipe as a guideline instead of something that must be strictly followed to the letter.

common elements

element	example	method
Fat	Olive oil, ghee, coconut oil	Heat the pot before adding the fat.
Aromatics*	Onions, carrots, celery, fennel	Sauté until softened or caramelized, from 3 to 15 minutes.
Dried herbs and spices*	Cumin, red pepper flakes, and even fresh garlic	Sauté for less than 1 minute.
Deglazing liquid	½ cup of broth or other liquid, such as wine or tamari	Simmer until reduced by half.
Main ingredients*	Vegetables, legumes, meat	Stir in to coat with the seasonings.
Broth	Broth or stock of choice	Bring to a boil, then simmer until the ingredients are soft enough to puree, cooked through, or at the desired tenderness.
Finishers	Salt, acid, garnishes, toppers	Taste, FASS (see page 22), then garnish and serve.

* Add a generous pinch of sea salt at these steps. Adding the salt throughout the cooking process allows it to penetrate into the vegetables, helping them release an abundant amount of flavor into your soup.

FASS = Fat + Acid + Salt + Sweet = YUM!

Soup-making is all about tasting throughout the cooking process, and FASS—which stands for fat, acid, salt, and sweet—is my easy tool for course-correcting soups as you taste them. If you've ever wondered how cooks elevate soups into the land of absolute yum, take a few minutes to learn all about FASS. It's time very well spent.

FASS

element	what it does	examples
Fat	Distributes flavor across the palate. Makes you feel satiated. Unlocks all of the fat-soluble vitamins that are in many vegetables so you can better absorb them.	Extra-virgin olive oil Coconut milk Ghee Silken Nut Cream (page 129)
Acid	Draws out and brightens flavors. Aside from providing a little punch, it will help balance a soup that is too sweet or salty. Increases absorption of minerals and stimulates digestion.	Lemon juice Lime juice Vinegar Fresh Soup Salsas (pages 132 and 133) Many Herb Drizzle (page 127)
Salt	Brings out the flavor of foods. Moves flavor to the front of the tongue, where it's best perceived. Improves appetite and balances the ratio of potassium, essential for energy and cellular metabolism.	Sea salt Tamari Fish sauce Crunchy Kale Crumbles (page 125) Crispy Shiitake Mushrooms (page 123)
Sweet	Tames harsh, sour, bitter, and spicy flavors. Rounds out or harmonizes flavors. Increases the desire to eat and the sense of pleasure.	Maple syrup* Coconut palm sugar Sweet potatoes

* The labeling for maple syrup is changing. The former Grade B (old system) is becoming Grade A: Dark Color & Robust Flavor. You want the darker syrup, which is harvested later in the season. It has a more concentrated flavor and is sweeter, so less is needed.

BUILDING AN INVENTORY FOR EVERYDAY EATING

Having a stash of broths in the freezer will help get soup into your menu rotation. In a pinch, frozen broth can become a satisfying soup in less than thirty minutes.

For example, if you make one broth every other week, for most of the broths that's six quarts or twenty-four cups, which could suffice for up to four soups. You can eat some and freeze some, creating your own little market right inside your freezer. If you're feeding a large family, double each recipe. This allows you to build an inventory of broths and soups that will help with your meal planning. When it comes to making broths, don't feel beholden to the stove top. Instead, try an electric pressure cooker, which speeds up the process, or a slow cooker, which you can turn on and forget about. If you establish a broth-making habit, you'll have plenty of opportunities to make a variety of soups.

nourishing broths

Want to know the difference between good soup and great soup? Homemade broth or stock. It's the rock-solid foundation on which fantastic soups are built. Musically, it's like laying down a great rhythm track around which you're going to riff a soaring song. All the basic flavor notes are there in the pot, along with a powerhouse nutritional backbeat; together, they combine to create a heady brew.

People tend to think that commercially made products are the same as homemade broths and stocks. In an emergency, perhaps, but once you've made your own, you'll never go store-bought again. The idea of controlling everything that goes into the pot is empowering, especially if revitalization is your goal. Then there is the exponential increase in flavor. The intoxicating taste of home-created broth, brought to fruition, will convince you that time invested in the kitchen makes for culinary adventures you will treasure and yearn to recreate.

These broth and stock recipes are incredibly versatile. They're designed to be interchangeable; your personal favorites, be they meat- or vegetable-based, will work with many of the soups in the book. They're also designed to be mini meals unto themselves. I know it's trendy now for certain restaurants to dispense bone and veggie broths out of walk-up windows, but honestly, I've been sipping broth for years (and I have the thermos to prove it). There's something immensely satisfying and satiating about imbibing a warming broth, knowing all the while that you're infusing vital nutrients into every cell in your body. Bone broths are phenomenal sources of amino acids such as glycine and proline, which are great for bone health, while other nutrients aid in digestion and healing the gut. Vegetable broths are mineral powerhouses, delivering such goodies as magnesium, potassium, calcium, and manganese—which is like taking your cells to a day at the spa!

broth and stock pairings

While you can use many of the recipes in this chapter for the soups in this book, this table presents the pairings I like best. As you become familiar with the recipes, you'll notice how each broth or stock punctuates a soup with different flavors.

magic mineral broth	thai coconut broth	chicken magic mineral broth	old-fashioned chicken stock	immune broth	nourishing bone broth	pastured beef bone broth
*						
*						
*		*				
*		*			*	*
*						
*				*		
*		*				
*						
	*					
	*					
*						
*		*	*			
*						
		*	*			
		*				
*						
*						
*		*	*			
*					*	*
			*			

	magic mineral broth	thai coconut broth	chicken magic mineral broth	old-fashioned chicken stock	immune broth	nourishing bone broth	pastured beef bone broth
	*						
	*						
	*						
	*	*					
			*	*			
	*			*		*	*
	*		*				
	*			*			
		*					
	*						
	*						
	*						
		*					
	*					*	*
	*		*	*			
	*						
				*			
	*					*	*
						*	*
	*						
	*						
	*			*			

making broth work for you

I mentioned versatility. The diagram at right is an example of one broth making four. You can take a full pot of Magic Mineral Broth (page 35). Freeze some. Take a couple of quarts and some roasted beef bones, put them in a slow cooker, and you have Pastured Beef Bone Broth (page 43). Take some more Magic Mineral Broth, infuse it with lemongrass, kaffir lime leaves, ginger, and coconut milk, and you have Thai Coconut Broth (page 36). Add chicken bones to Magic Mineral Broth, simmer, and the result is delicious Chicken Magic Mineral Broth (page 38). If you want to swap one of these out for a super immune-boosting fix, infuse the Magic Mineral Broth with shiitake mushrooms, ginger, and burdock root and you have my Immune Broth (page 40).

8 cups Magic Mineral Broth

2 (14.5-ounce) cans coconut milk

1 stalk lemongrass

3 kaffir lime leaves

3 (1-inch) pieces ginger

2 shallots

8 cups Magic Mineral Broth

½ fennel bulb

3 fresh shiitake mushrooms

1 (5-inch) piece burdock
root, scrubbed

3 sprigs
fresh thyme

1 (2-inch)) piece
fresh ginger

creates thai coconut broth

creates immune broth

magic
mineral
broth

creates chicken magic mineral broth

creates pastured beef bone broth

8 cups Magic
Mineral Broth

½ to 1 organic chicken carcass,
or 2 pounds chicken bones

8 cups Magic
Mineral Broth

1 pound roasted
beef marrow bones

cook's note: Simmer the Immune Broth, covered, for 2 hours; simmer the Thai Coconut Broth, covered, for 50 minutes; and simmer the Chicken Magic Mineral Broth and Pastured Beef Bone Broth, covered, for 4 hours.

magic mineral broth

makes about 6 quarts | prep time: 10 minutes | cook time: 2 to 3 hours

This is my signature savory broth. Its creation was that wonderful moment when everything came together in the kitchen to create something truly healing. (I must have been channeling someone's grandmother!) Literally thousands of people have spoken with me about the positive impact this broth has had on their lives. You'll be amazed at how revitalizing it is. With carrots, onions, leek, celery, potatoes, and more, it's a veritable veggie-palooza and can be used as a base for nearly all the soups in this book. In a bowl or sipped as a tea, it's the perfect cleansing broth.

6 unpeeled carrots, cut into thirds

2 unpeeled yellow onions, quartered

1 leek, white and green parts, cut into thirds

1 bunch celery, including the heart, cut into thirds

4 unpeeled red potatoes, quartered

2 unpeeled Japanese or regular sweet potatoes, quartered

1 unpeeled garnet yam (sweet potato), quartered

5 unpeeled cloves garlic, halved

½ bunch fresh flat-leaf parsley

1 (8-inch) strip kombu

12 black peppercorns

4 whole allspice or juniper berries

2 bay leaves

8 quarts cold, filtered water, plus more if needed

1 teaspoon sea salt, plus more if needed

Rinse all of the vegetables well, including the kombu.

In a 12-quart or larger stockpot, combine the carrots, onions, leek, celery, red potatoes, sweet potatoes, yam, garlic, parsley, kombu, peppercorns, allspice berries, and bay leaves. Add the water, cover, and bring to a boil over high heat. Decrease the heat to low and simmer, partially covered, for at least 2 hours, or until the full richness of the vegetables can be tasted. As the broth simmers, some of the water will evaporate; add more if the vegetables begin to peek out.

Strain the broth through a large, coarse-mesh sieve (use a heat-resistant container underneath), and discard the solids. Stir in the salt, adding more if desired. Let cool to room temperature before refrigerating or freezing. Store in the refrigerator for up to 5 days or in the freezer for up to 6 months.

thai coconut broth

makes about 3 quarts | prep time: 15 minutes | cook time: 50 minutes

Am I allowed to say I love this broth? This is like taking your taste buds on a trip to Thailand—infusing Magic Mineral Broth or, if you prefer, chicken broth with lemongrass, ginger, shallots, kaffir lime leaves, and coconut milk. There are nutrients galore, notably in the coconut milk, which contains good fats and the same immune-boosting, antiviral lauric acid that's found in breast milk. The taste is both bright and remarkably comforting.

8 cups Magic Mineral Broth (page 35) or Chicken Magic Mineral Broth (page 38)

2 (14.5-ounce) cans coconut milk

3 (1-inch) pieces fresh ginger

2 shallots, peeled and halved

3 kaffir lime leaves, or 1 teaspoon lime zest

1 stalk lemongrass, cut in chunks and bruised

¼ teaspoon sea salt, plus more if needed

In a 6-quart pot, combine the broth, coconut milk, ginger, shallots, lime leaves, lemongrass, and ¼ teaspoon salt and bring to a low boil over medium heat. Cook for about 20 minutes. Decrease the heat to low and let the broth simmer for another 30 minutes. Remove the ginger, shallots, lime leaves, and lemongrass with a slotted spoon. Taste and add more salt if desired.

Let cool to room temperature before refrigerating or freezing. Store in the refrigerator for up to 5 days or in the freezer for up to 6 months.

chicken magic mineral broth

makes about 6 quarts | prep time: 10 minutes | cook time: 2 to 4 hours

From a taste and nutrition perspective, adding chicken bones to Magic Mineral Broth really kicks everything into overdrive. A hit of freshly squeezed lemon juice (or white or apple cider vinegar) is added to encourage the bones to give up their essential calcium and phosphorus. If you're worried about your bones—and who isn't?—this is a fantastic broth. If there's a little meat on the bones, so much the better: chicken is a great source of protein and niacin, which produces something most of us want—energy. As for the flavor, let's just say you're in for a palate full of pleasure.

6 unpeeled carrots, cut into thirds

2 unpeeled yellow onions, quartered

2 leeks, white and green parts, cut into thirds

1 bunch celery, including the heart, cut into thirds

4 unpeeled red potatoes, quartered

2 unpeeled Japanese or regular sweet potatoes, quartered

1 unpeeled garnet yam (sweet potato), quartered

8 unpeeled cloves garlic, halved

1 bunch fresh flat-leaf parsley

1 (8-inch) strip kombu

12 black peppercorns

4 whole allspice or juniper berries

2 bay leaves

1 tablespoon freshly squeezed lemon juice or white or apple cider vinegar

1 organic chicken carcass, or 2 pounds chicken bones

8 quarts cold, filtered water, plus more if needed

Sea salt

Rinse all of the vegetables well, including the kombu.

In a 12- to 16-quart stockpot, combine the carrots, onions, leeks, celery, red potatoes, sweet potatoes, yam, garlic, parsley, kombu, peppercorns, allspice, bay leaves, lemon juice, and chicken carcass. Add the water, filling the pot to 2 inches below the rim. Cover, and bring to a boil over high heat. Remove the lid, decrease the heat to low, and skim off the scum that has risen to the top. Simmer, partially covered, for at least 2 hours. As the broth simmers, some of the water will evaporate; add more if the vegetables begin to peek out. Simmer until the bones begin to soften and fall apart, about 4 hours, or as long as you're willing to let it simmer away.

Strain the broth through a large, coarse-mesh sieve, then stir in salt to taste. Let cool to room temperature, then refrigerate overnight. Skim off as much fat as you can from the top of the broth (see Cook's Note), then portion into airtight containers. Store in the refrigerator for up to 5 days or in the freezer for up to 6 months.

cook's note: Here's a trick from Ma's kitchen: once you've skimmed the fat from the surface of the broth, you can remove even more by dabbing the surface of the broth with paper towels to sop it up.

old-fashioned chicken stock

makes about 6 quarts | prep time: 10 minutes | cook time: 3 hours

Some things you learn at your father's knee. But chicken stock? I learned that at my mother's elbow, watching from my perch on the yellow Formica kitchen countertop as she reenacted her Nana's chicken stock note by note. Onions, carrots, celery, chicken . . . it's down-home, old-time comfort in a pot. I can't think of a better way to get vital nutrients, with a flavor that will leave you longing for more.

6 pounds organic chicken backs, necks, bones, and wings

2 unpeeled white onions, quartered

4 unpeeled large carrots, cut into thirds

2 stalks celery, cut in thirds

6 sprigs fresh thyme

4 unpeeled cloves garlic, halved

1 large bunch fresh flat-leaf parsley

1 bay leaf

8 black peppercorns

8 quarts cold, filtered water, plus more if needed

Sea salt

cook's note: The stock will cool faster in smaller containers. Make sure it's refrigerated within 4 hours of cooking.

Rinse all of the vegetables well.

In a 12-quart or larger stockpot, combine the chicken, onions, carrots, celery, thyme, garlic, parsley, bay leaf, and peppercorns. Add the water, cover, and cook over medium-high heat until the water comes to a boil. Decrease the heat so the bubbles just break the surface of the liquid. Skim off the scum and fat that have risen to the surface. Simmer, partially covered, for about 3 hours. Add more water if the vegetables begin to peek out.

Strain the stock through a fine-mesh sieve or colander lined with unbleached cheesecloth into a clean pot or heat-resistant bowl, then stir salt in to taste. Bring to room temperature, then store in an airtight container in the refrigerator. Skim off as much fat as you can from the top of the broth, then portion into airtight containers. Store in the refrigerator for up to 5 days or in the freezer for up to 6 months.

immune broth

makes about 4 quarts | prep time: 15 minutes | cook time: 90 minutes

Whether you're under the weather or just looking for an immunity boost, this is a great go-to broth. Here I introduce you to burdock root. It's loaded with potassium, iron, magnesium, and ever-important zinc. In the olden days, physicians used burdock root as a blood purifier, and clearly science has shown they were onto something. Here I combine burdock with shiitake mushrooms, ginger, and garlic to create a delicious earthy broth that's full of antiviral, antimicrobial, and anti-inflammatory goodness.

1 fennel bulb plus stalks, cut into chunks

1 unpeeled yellow onion, quartered

3 unpeeled carrots, cut into thirds

½ bunch celery, including the heart, cut into thirds

1 sweet potato, cut into chunks

½ large bunch fresh flat-leaf parsley

6 fresh shiitake mushrooms

1 (3-inch) piece burdock root, quartered crosswise

6 sprigs fresh thyme

6 large unpeeled cloves garlic, halved

1 (2-inch) piece fresh ginger, halved lengthwise

1 (8-inch) strip kombu

6 black peppercorns

1 bay leaf

4 quarts cold, filtered water, plus more if needed

2 teaspoons sea salt, plus more if needed

Rinse all of the vegetables well, including the kombu.

In a 6-quart or larger stockpot, combine the fennel, onion, carrots, celery, sweet potato, parsley, shiitakes, burdock root, thyme, garlic, ginger, kombu, peppercorns, and bay leaf. Add the water, cover, and bring to a boil over high heat. Decrease the heat to low and simmer, partially covered, for at least 90 minutes, or until the full richness of the vegetables can be tasted. As the broth simmers, some of the water will evaporate; add more if the vegetables begin to peek out.

Strain the broth through a large, coarse-mesh sieve (use a heat-resistant container underneath). Stir in the salt, adding more to taste if desired. Let cool to room temperature before refrigerating or freezing. Store in the refrigerator for up to 5 days or in the freezer for up to 6 months.

variation: For an immunity and anti-inflammatory boost, add 3 (1-inch) slices of fresh turmeric root or 1½ teaspoons ground turmeric during the last 30 minutes of cooking.

nourishing bone broth

makes about 6 quarts | prep time: 25 minutes | cook time: 8 to 16 hours

Put this one in the time machine. Bone broths are trendy these days, but in fact they've been around since the ancient Greeks. It turns out the gelatin that seeps from the bones as they simmer is great for gut health and digestion. Beef bones also contain high amounts of calcium and magnesium, which are great for your bones. One note: invest in pasture-raised, organic bones if at all possible, to ensure you're getting the highest-quality ingredients possible, free of hormones and antibiotics.

3 pounds marrow bones from grass-fed organic beef or chicken bones

3 unpeeled carrots, cut into thirds

2 unpeeled yellow onions, quartered

1 bunch celery, including the heart, cut into thirds

5 unpeeled cloves garlic, halved

½ bunch fresh flat-leaf parsley

12 black peppercorns

2 bay leaves

4 sprigs fresh thyme

1 tablespoon apple cider vinegar

8 quarts cold, filtered water, plus more if needed

Sea salt

Preheat the oven to 425°F.

Place the bones on a rimmed baking sheet or roasting pan and roast until browned, 20 to 30 minutes.

Rinse all of the vegetables well. In a 12-quart or larger stockpot, combine the bones, carrots, onions, celery, garlic, parsley, peppercorns, bay leaves, thyme, and vinegar. Pour in the water, cover, and bring to a boil over high heat. Remove the lid, decrease the heat to low, and skim off the scum that has risen to the top. Simmer gently, partially covered, for 8 to 16 hours (or use my slow cooker shortcut, page 43). As the broth simmers, some of the water will evaporate; add more if the vegetables begin to peek out.

Remove and discard the bones, then strain the broth through a large, coarse-mesh sieve; stir in the salt to taste. Let cool to room temperature, and then refrigerate overnight in an airtight container. Skim off as much fat as you can from the top of the broth, then portion into airtight containers. Store in the refrigerator for up to 5 days or in the freezer for up to 6 months.

pastured beef bone broth

makes about 6 quarts | prep time: 25 minutes | cook time: 8 to 24 hours

If broth could be compared to wine, I'd describe this beef bone broth as the equivalent of a big Cabernet. Yes, it has that much heartiness. Go for grass-fed beef here since it has the best nutritional and taste profile, and then surround dem bones with all sorts of vegetables and herbs. Parsley, allspice, bay leaves, and garlic create a heady smell and rich flavor that can be enjoyed again and again. In fact, many people use bone broth as a tea, sipping it as a bracing, warm tonic throughout the day.

3 pounds marrow bones from grass-fed organic beef

6 unpeeled carrots, cut into thirds

2 unpeeled yellow onions, quartered

1 leek, white and green parts, cut into thirds

1 bunch celery, including the heart, cut into thirds

5 unpeeled cloves garlic, halved

½ bunch fresh flat-leaf parsley

4 unpeeled red potatoes, quartered

2 unpeeled Japanese or regular sweet potatoes, quartered

1 unpeeled garnet yam (sweet potato), quartered

1 (8-inch) strip of kombu

2 bay leaves

12 black peppercorns

4 whole allspice or juniper berries

1 tablespoon apple cider vinegar

8 quarts cold, filtered water, plus more if needed

1 teaspoon sea salt

Preheat the oven to 425°F.

Place the bones on a rimmed baking sheet or roasting pan and roast until well browned, about 30 minutes.

Rinse all of the vegetables well, including the kombu. In a 12-quart or larger stockpot, combine the bones, carrots, onions, leek, celery, garlic, parsley, red potatoes, sweet potatoes, yam, kombu, bay leaves, peppercorns, allspice berries, and vinegar. Pour in the water, cover, and bring to a boil over high heat. Remove the lid, decrease the heat to low, and skim off the scum that has risen to the top. Simmer gently, partially covered, for 8 to 24 hours. As the broth simmers, some of the water will evaporate; add more if the vegetables begin to peek out.

Remove and discard the bones, then strain the broth through a large, coarse-mesh sieve. Stir in the salt. Let cool to room temperature, and then refrigerate overnight in an airtight container. Skim off as much fat as you can from the top of the broth, then portion into airtight containers. Store in the refrigerator for up to 5 days or in the freezer for up to 6 months.

cook's note: To make a shortcut version, roast the bones as directed and place in a 6-quart slow cooker. Cover with about 8 cups of Magic Mineral Broth (page 35) and add the vinegar. Set the slow cooker on low and cook for 8 to 12 hours, allowing the broth to simmer quietly. Strain the broth, cool, pour into an airtight container, and refrigerate overnight. Skim off the fat and add 2 more quarts of Magical Mineral Broth.

blended soups

I like to call blended soups "cashmere soups." What, you ask, is a cashmere soup? It's simply the most velvety soup imaginable, made possible by blending vegetables with a high-speed or immersion blender after they've gone through the cooking process. All that air whipped into the mix yields a beautiful texture and provides a completely satiating culinary experience. Aside from creating a sumptuous taste sensation, the blending also predigests the ingredients. This is important for enhancing detoxification as it gives your digestive system and other internal organs a break.

Versatility is the hallmark of these cashmere soups. Some people, myself included, like to have a little something to chew on with their soup. If you fall into this category, you don't have to blend all of the soup. Try blending only half; that will give you a cozy blanket over a bed of delightful veggies. Or if you prefer, you can add one of the toppers (see page 119), which give a stellar finish to soups. So whether you fall into the smooth and creamy crew or the crispy and crunchy crowd, each of these cashmere soups can be adapted to your taste preference.

Most of us are also visual eaters—no one wants to eat something that looks like a swamp—and these soups are an absolute feast for the eyes. They remind me of a vibrant Peter Max painting, rolling through every radii of the Pantone color wheel. Bright colors are a sure sign of high antioxidant properties (see, there really is something to eating the rainbow!), and other great nutrients as well. The reds, oranges, and greens will astonish your senses and draw you almost hypnotically to these soups. What I love about these cashmere soups is how they give you so much bang for the nutritional buck. There's no way, in raw form, that you'd ever be able to consume the amount of greens you'll find in some of these soups. Yet the very act of blending and cooking allows you to break it all down and create nutrient- and flavor-dense soups that pack a wallop. Listen closely and that sound you'll hear will be your cells thanking you for taking such good care of them!

roasted apple and butternut squash soup

makes 6 servings | prep time: 15 minutes | cook time: 40 minutes

If it's possible for a soup to remind you of pie, this one pulls off the trick. This is a cross between apple and pumpkin pie. Your olfactory sense is going to go off the rails as the chopped apple and squash roast, assisted by the warming notes of allspice and cinnamon. Add a little walnut cream to the doled-out soup at the end, and it's like adding ice cream to your pie—a stunner.

2 tablespoons extra-virgin olive oil

Sea salt

1 teaspoon ground allspice

½ teaspoon ground cinnamon

2 unpeeled apples, rinsed and cut into 1-inch cubes

1 pound butternut squash, peeled, seeded, and cut into 1-inch cubes (see Cook's Note)

6 cups Magic Mineral Broth (page 35)

¼ teaspoon freshly ground black pepper

1 tablespoon freshly squeezed lemon juice, plus more if needed

¼ cup Silken Nut Cream (page 129), preferably made with walnuts

Preheat the oven to 400°F. Line a baking sheet with parchment paper.

In a large bowl, combine the olive oil, ¼ teaspoon salt, the allspice, and cinnamon and stir until well combined. Add the apples and butternut squash and toss with the spice mixture until evenly coated. Place the seasoned vegetables in a single layer on the prepared baking sheet and roast for 25 minutes, or until tender.

Pour one-third of the broth into a blender, add one-third of the apples and squash, and blend until smooth, adding more broth as needed. Transfer to a soup pot over low heat and repeat the process two more times with the remaining broth and roasted apples and squash. Stir in any remaining broth, along with ¼ teaspoon salt and the pepper and lemon juice. Taste; you may want to add another spritz of lemon juice or a pinch of salt. Serve topped with nut cream, or store in an airtight container in the refrigerator for up to 5 days or in the freezer for up to 3 months.

cook's note: If you don't want to take out your chainsaw, many grocers have done the heavy lifting for you. Look for precut butternut squash cubes in the produce section.

avocado citrus soup

makes 6 servings | prep time: 10 minutes | cook time: none

Avocado demands a citrus accompaniment. I could have gone in a Latin direction (think guacamole), but I opted for something more in the arena of salad-in-a-blender (sounds strange, but it works). Lemon, orange, arugula, and basil combine with the front and forward taste of the avocado to create a creamy, luscious, satiating chilled soup.

4½ cups Magic Mineral Broth (page 35)

3 avocados, halved and pitted

1 teaspoon sea salt

2 tablespoons extra-virgin olive oil

1 clove garlic, chopped

2 teaspoons lemon zest

2 tablespoons freshly squeezed lemon juice

2 tablespoons freshly squeezed orange juice

1 cup tightly packed baby arugula

1 tablespoon chopped fresh basil

2 teaspoons chopped fresh mint

¼ cup Many Herb Drizzle (page 127), for garnish

6 tablespoons Avocado and Cucumber Salsa (page 132), for garnish

Put the broth, avocados, salt, olive oil, garlic, lemon zest, lemon juice, orange juice, and arugula in a blender and process until smooth. Add the basil and mint and blend just until combined. Refrigerate for at least 2 hours, until chilled. Serve in small bowls, garnished with the drizzle and salsa, or store in an airtight container in the refrigerator for up to 5 days or in the freezer for up to 3 months.

springtime asparagus and leek soup

makes 6 servings | prep time: 15 minutes | cook time: 20 minutes

I know spring is just around the corner when asparagus makes its annual appearance at the farmers' market. Here I've paired it with another harbinger of longer days, leek, and added garlic and fennel. Sautéing imparts a brilliant emerald green color to the asparagus, and blending eliminates the vegetable's usual stringiness. The parsley and dill crank up the herbaceous nature of the soup, as well as imparting their own complementary shades of verde to the mix. In all, it's a joyous fusion—and a culinary ode to my favorite season of the year.

2 tablespoons extra-virgin olive oil

1 large leek, white part only, rinsed and finely chopped

Sea salt

1 fennel bulb, chopped

1 clove garlic, minced

2 pounds asparagus, tough ends snapped off, cut into ½-inch pieces

6 cups Old-Fashioned Chicken Stock (page 39) or Magic Mineral Broth (page 35)

¼ teaspoon freshly ground black pepper

¼ cup finely chopped fresh flat-leaf parsley

1 tablespoon chopped fresh dill

1 tablespoon freshly squeezed lemon juice, plus more if needed

½ teaspoon lemon zest

Heat the olive oil in a soup pot over medium heat, then add the leek and a pinch of salt and sauté just until translucent, about 3 minutes. Add the fennel and sauté 3 minutes more. Stir in the garlic, asparagus, and ¼ teaspoon salt. Pour in 1 cup of the stock, cover, and cook until the asparagus is just tender and emerald green, about 2 minutes, or a bit longer for thicker stalks. Remove from the heat.

Pour one-third of the remaining stock into a blender and add one-third of the vegetable mixture. Blend until smooth. Transfer to a soup pot over low heat. Repeat the process two more times. Stir in the pepper, parsley, dill, lemon juice, lemon zest, and ¼ teaspoon salt. Taste and adjust with an additional squeeze of lemon and a couple of pinches of salt if needed. Store in an airtight container in the refrigerator for up to 5 days or in the freezer for up to 3 months.

moroccan carrot soup

makes 6 servings | prep time: 15 minutes | cook time: 30 minutes

Saffron is one of my favorite spices to cook with. Yes, it can be a bit costly, but you really need very little saffron to get a huge bang for your buck. Here it gives a luscious, exotic taste to the carrots, which are naturally sweet. Saffron is also a visual delight; in this soup the saffron looks like monks' robes tossed against a vibrant orange background. Consider this dish a treat for all your senses.

2 tablespoons extra-virgin olive oil

1 yellow onion, chopped

Sea salt

3 pounds carrots, cut into 1-inch pieces

1 teaspoon ground cumin

½ teaspoon ground coriander

½ teaspoon ground cinnamon

Pinch of red pepper flakes

½ teaspoon saffron threads

6 cups Magic Mineral Broth (page 35), Chicken Magic Mineral Broth (page 38), or Nourishing Bone Broth (page 41), plus more if needed

2½ teaspoons Meyer lemon zest (See Cook's Note)

1 tablespoon freshly squeezed Meyer lemon juice, plus more if needed (See Cook's Note)

¼ teaspoon dark maple syrup, plus more if needed

Chermoula (page 122), for garnish (optional)

Heat the olive oil in a soup pot over medium heat, then add the onion and a pinch of salt and sauté until golden, about 4 minutes. Stir in the carrots, cumin, coriander, cinnamon, red pepper flakes, saffron, and ¼ teaspoon salt and sauté until well combined. Pour in ½ cup of the broth and cook until the liquid is reduced by half. Add the remaining 5½ cups of broth and another ¼ teaspoon salt and cook until the carrots are tender, about 20 minutes.

Put the lemon zest in a blender and puree the soup in batches until very smooth, each time adding the cooking liquid first and then the carrot mixture. If need be, add additional broth to reach the desired thickness. Return the soup to the pot over low heat, stir in the lemon juice, maple syrup, and a pinch of salt, and gently reheat. Taste; you may want to add another squeeze of lemon, a pinch or two of salt, or a drizzle of maple syrup. Serve with chermoula or store in an airtight container in the refrigerator for up to 5 days or in the freezer for up to 3 months.

cook's note: Meyer lemons are milder and sweeter than most store-bought lemons. If you don't have Meyer lemons, use 2 teaspoons of lemon juice combined with 2 teaspoons of freshly squeezed tangerine or orange juice. As for the zest, regular lemon zest is an acceptable substitute.

greek cucumber yogurt soup

makes 6 servings | prep time: 10 minutes | cook time: none

If this immediately brings to mind Greek tzatziki sauce, well, that's what it was designed to do. I love tzatziki—it's so cool and refreshing—and I figured if it was good enough for a sauce, it would work great as a chilled soup. And so it goes. Normally with tzatziki you have to grate those hydrating cucumbers. With this recipe, everything goes in the blender—*and boom!*—you have soup. The only thing you have to do is put it in the fridge to cool. It's absolutely luscious on a hot day.

2 cups full-fat plain yogurt

2 English cucumbers, peeled, seeded, and coarsely chopped

1 clove garlic, chopped

1 teaspoon lemon zest

1 tablespoon freshly squeezed lemon juice

1 teaspoon sea salt

¼ teaspoon freshly ground black pepper

½ teaspoon ground coriander

1 teaspoon chopped fresh mint

1 teaspoon dark maple syrup

6 tablespoons Many Herb Drizzle (page 127) or 6 tablespoons Avocado and Cucumber Salsa (page 132), for garnish

Put the yogurt, cucumbers, garlic, lemon zest, lemon juice, salt, pepper, coriander, mint, and maple syrup in a blender and process until smooth. Refrigerate for at least 2 hours, until chilled. Serve in small bowls, garnished with the drizzle, or store in an airtight container in the refrigerator for up to 5 days or in the freezer for up to 3 months.

not your average gazpacho

makes 6 servings | prep time: 20 minutes | cook time: none

This take on gazpacho, topped with avocado salsa, is revitalization in a cup (or shot glass; I love serving this up as a shooter). Most gazpachos are chunky and you need ninja knife skills to negotiate the recipe, but here all the ingredients get a quick chop and then are thrown in the blender. Even the most novice soup-makers will find this recipe is nearly effortless. I've riffed a bit off traditional gazpacho, adding fennel, celery, cumin, and coriander to the mix, and the end result is absolutely mouthwatering!

3 cups low-sodium tomato juice

¼ cup extra-virgin olive oil

1 tablespoon plus 1 teaspoon freshly squeezed lemon juice

1 tablespoon dark maple syrup, plus more if needed

1 teaspoon sea salt, plus more if needed

½ teaspoon ground cumin

¼ teaspoon ground coriander

⅛ teaspoon cayenne pepper

2 cloves garlic, coarsely chopped

1 fennel bulb, quartered and cored

3 stalks celery, coarsely chopped

1 English cucumber, peeled, seeded, and coarsely chopped

1 red bell pepper, coarsely chopped

2 cups cherry tomatoes

1 small red onion, coarsely chopped

¼ cup coarsely chopped fresh basil, cilantro, or a combination

6 tablespoons Avocado and Cucumber Salsa (page 132), for garnish

Put the tomato juice, olive oil, lemon juice, maple syrup, salt, cumin, coriander, cayenne, garlic, fennel, celery, cucumber, bell pepper, tomatoes, onion, and basil in a large bowl and stir to combine. Working in batches, transfer to a blender and process until completely smooth. Taste; you may want to add a pinch of salt or a bit of maple syrup. Serve in small glasses, garnished with the salsa, or store in an airtight container in the refrigerator for up to 5 days or in the freezer for up to 3 months.

chilled watermelon soup with chile and lime

makes 6 servings | prep time: 15 minutes | cook time: none

The last thing you want to do on a steamy day is turn on the burners in the kitchen. That's where this chilled soup comes in. Watermelon is so refreshing and hydrating (not to mention it's full of the outstanding antioxidant lycopene) that it's the perfect summertime soup. I know at first glance that adding olive oil and jalapeños to the mix might seem strange, but you have to trust me on this: the oil makes the soup more satiating, while the jalapeño kick blends deliciously with the sweet of the watermelon. The mint provides an ideal high note; I make sure to put it in after everything else has blended, and I only hit the pulse button once or twice so the mint doesn't lose its character. A little of this soup goes a long way. I like to serve it in jelly jars or fun glasses with a small garnish of watermelon rind.

4 cups seeded watermelon chunks

2 tablespoons extra-virgin olive oil

1 small jalapeño pepper, seeded and chopped

1 teaspoon honey

1 teaspoon lime zest

3 tablespoons freshly squeezed lime juice

1 teaspoon sea salt

10 ice cubes

1 tablespoon chopped fresh mint

6 sprigs fresh mint, for garnish

Put the watermelon, olive oil, jalapeño, honey, lime zest, lime juice, salt, and ice cubes in a blender and process until smooth. Add the chopped mint and blend just until combined. Serve in glasses, garnished with the mint sprigs. This soup tastes best the day it is made.

cook's note: The ice cubes will chill the soup, so it can be eaten immediately. However, if you want it super chilled, cover and refrigerate for 1 hour before serving.

silk road pumpkin soup

makes 6 servings | prep time: 15 minutes | cook time: 45 minutes

Kabocha isn't as sweet as butternut squash, but it has a lovely, nutty taste. It also smells like heaven when it's roasting. Paired with parsnips, it makes this soup a fiber powerhouse, proving that fiber-rich foods are far from tasteless.

4 tablespoons extra-virgin olive oil

Sea salt

¼ teaspoon ground allspice

½ teaspoon ground cinnamon

½ teaspoon ground cardamom

2½ pounds kabocha squash, quartered and seeded

1 yellow onion, diced

2 parsnips, diced small

2 cloves garlic, minced

1 tablespoon minced fresh ginger

6 cups Magic Mineral Broth (page 35), plus more if needed

2 teaspoons freshly squeezed lemon juice, plus more if needed

Preheat the oven to 400°F. Line a baking sheet with parchment paper.

In a small bowl combine 2 tablespoons of the olive oil, ¼ teaspoon salt, the allspice, ¼ teaspoon of the cinnamon, and ¼ teaspoon of the cardamom. Rub the spice mixture into the cut sides of the squash. Place the squash on the prepared baking sheet and roast for 30 minutes, until tender.

While the squash is roasting, heat the remaining 2 tablespoons of olive oil in a soup pot over medium-high heat, then add the onion, parsnips, and ¼ teaspoon salt and sauté until golden and translucent, about 6 minutes. Add the remaining ¼ teaspoon of cinnamon, the remaining ¼ teaspoon of cardamom, and the garlic and ginger and sauté until fragrant, about 30 seconds more. Pour in 1 cup of the broth to deglaze the pot, stirring to loosen any bits stuck to the bottom. Remove from the heat. When the squash has cooled to the touch, scoop the flesh into the pot with the vegetables. Put one-third of the remaining broth and one-third of the vegetables into a blender and blend until smooth, adding more liquid as needed. Transfer to a soup pot over low heat and repeat the process two more times. Stir in a ½ teaspoon salt and the lemon juice. Taste; you may want to add another spritz of lemon juice or a pinch of salt. Store in an airtight container in the refrigerator for up to 5 days or in the freezer for up to 3 months.

power green soup

makes 6 servings | prep time: 15 minutes | cook time: 25 minutes

If a soup could do push-ups, this one would. Nearly nuclear in terms of energy, there's hardly a vitamin or mineral out there that can't be found among the kale, chard, leek, fennel, garlic, and shiitake mushroom base of the Immune Broth. The challenge here was making a green soup that tasted delicious. I think this one passes with flying colors, highlighted by the gremolata topper.

2 tablespoons extra-virgin olive oil, plus more for drizzling

1 yellow onion, chopped

Sea salt

1 large leek, white parts only, rinsed and chopped

1 Yukon gold or Yellow Finn potato, peeled and diced small

2 cloves garlic, minced

¼ teaspoon red pepper flakes or freshly ground black pepper

6 cups Immune Broth (page 40) or Magic Mineral Broth (page 35)

1 bunch Swiss chard, stemmed and coarsely chopped

1 bunch dinosaur kale, stemmed and coarsely chopped

¼ cup loosely packed chopped fresh flat-leaf parsley

1 teaspoon lemon zest

1 tablespoon freshly squeezed lemon juice

Kale Gremolata (page 128) for garnish (optional) or Crunchy Kale Crumbles (page 125)

Heat the olive oil in a soup pot over medium heat, then add the onion and ¼ teaspoon salt and sauté until the onion is golden, about 10 minutes. Add the leek and potato and sauté for 3 minutes more. Add the garlic and red pepper flakes and stir for another 30 seconds. Pour in ½ cup of the broth, stirring to loosen any bits stuck to the pot, and cook until the liquid is reduced by half. Add the chard, kale, and another ¼ teaspoon salt. Stir well to combine so the greens will wilt. Then add the remaining 5½ cups of broth and bring to a boil. Cover, and simmer for 5 minutes, or until the greens are just tender.

In a blender, puree the soup in batches until very smooth, each time adding the cooking liquid first and then the greens. Blend the parsley into the last batch. Pour the soup back into the pot, heat gently over medium-low heat, and stir in the lemon zest and juice. Taste; you may want to add a pinch more salt. Serve garnished with a drizzle of olive oil and topped with the gremolata, or store in an airtight container in the refrigerator for up to 5 days or in the freezer for up to 3 months.

gingery broccoli soup with mint

makes 6 servings | prep time: 15 minutes | cook time: 20 minutes

The great thing about soup is that you can really stack the deck with a flavor you're intent on bringing forth. I was looking for a lot of sparkle in this blend, a really *big*-tasting soup, and I found it with a huge hit of mint and ginger. Plus, for people intent on a plant-centric diet, spices and herbs count (hey, they're plants) and are full of healing phytonutrients and anti-inflammatory riches. If you're looking for a substitute for mint, try basil; it's a member of the mint family and provides a complementary taste.

2 tablespoons extra-virgin olive oil, plus more for drizzling

1 yellow onion, chopped

Sea salt

2 cloves garlic, minced

3 tablespoons grated fresh ginger

⅛ teaspoon red pepper flakes

6 cups Magic Mineral Broth (page 35) or Chicken Magic Mineral Broth (page 38)

2 pounds broccoli, cut into florets, stems peeled and cut into small chunks

½ cup loosely packed, chopped fresh flat-leaf parsley

2 teaspoons chopped fresh mint

1 teaspoon lemon zest

2 tablespoons freshly squeezed lemon juice

1 teaspoon dark maple syrup

Heat the olive oil in a soup pot over medium heat, then add the onion and a pinch of salt and sauté just until golden, about 5 minutes. Add the garlic, ginger, and red pepper flakes. Continue sautéing for 1 minute, until aromatic. Add the broth, cover, and bring to a boil. Stir in the broccoli and ½ teaspoon salt and cook for 2 minutes, or until the broccoli turns bright green.

In a blender, combine one-third of the broth and one-third of the vegetables. Blend until smooth. Pour into a clean pot and repeat with another one-third of the broth and the broccoli. Then blend the remaining broth and broccoli with the parsley, mint, lemon zest, lemon juice, maple syrup, and ¼ teaspoon salt. Pour into the soup pot and stir. Reheat the soup very slowly over low heat. Taste; you may want to add a pinch or two of salt. Serve garnished with a drizzle of olive oil, or store in an airtight container in the refrigerator for up to 5 days or in the freezer for up to 3 months.

golden beet and fennel soup

makes 6 servings | prep time: 20 minutes | cook time: 35 minutes

You read the title of this recipe correctly: beets don't just come in deep, rich colors, but golden as well. Unlike their earthy-tasting cousins, golden beets are mellower and sweeter. Their medicinal use is legendary: the ancient Assyrians grew them in the Hanging Gardens of Babylon and ate them for better health. I paired golden beets with fennel because they grow together, and one of the maxims in soup-making is what grows together goes together. Fennel, when sautéed, is sweet while retaining a slight anise flavor. I also include a little ginger, resulting in a nice, gentle soup that's easy on the constitution.

3 tablespoons extra-virgin olive oil

1 yellow onion, diced

2 carrots, peeled and diced

1 fennel bulb, diced

Sea salt

1 tablespoon grated fresh ginger

1 pound golden beets, peeled and diced

6 cups Magic Mineral Broth (page 35)

½ teaspoon orange zest

3 tablespoons freshly squeezed orange juice

1 tablespoon freshly squeezed lemon juice

1 tablespoon chopped fresh mint, for garnish

Heat the olive oil in a soup pot over medium heat, then add the onion, carrots, fennel, and ½ teaspoon salt and sauté until golden, about 6 minutes. Stir in the ginger and beets and sauté until well combined and well coated. Pour in ½ cup of the broth to deglaze the pot, stirring to loosen any bits stuck to the bottom, and cook until the liquid is reduced by half.

Add the remaining 5½ cups of broth and another ½ teaspoon salt. Bring to a boil, then cover and simmer until the beets are tender, 20 to 25 minutes.

In a blender, puree the soup in batches until very smooth, each time adding the cooking liquid first and then the beet mixture. Pour the soup back into the pot, heat gently, and stir in the orange zest, orange juice, and lemon juice. Taste; you may want to add a pinch more salt. Serve garnished with the mint, or store in an airtight container in the refrigerator for up to 5 days or in the freezer for up to 3 months.

coconut cauliflower soup with ginger and turmeric

makes 6 servings | prep time: 20 minutes | cook time: 35 minutes

Roasting cauliflower brings out the vegetable's natural sweetness and creates a beautiful golden brown color that delights the eyes as much as the taste buds. Add Thai coconut and the taste is divine!

2½ to 3 pounds cauliflower, cut into 1½-inch florets

3 tablespoons extra-virgin olive oil

½ teaspoon ground turmeric

Sea salt

¼ teaspoon freshly ground black pepper

1 yellow onion, chopped

2 cloves garlic, minced

2 carrots, peeled and chopped

2 stalks celery, chopped

2 teaspoons Thai red chili paste

6 cups Thai Coconut Broth (page 36), plus more if needed

2 teaspoons grated fresh ginger

1 tablespoon freshly squeezed lime juice, plus more if needed

1 tablespoon finely chopped fresh mint or cilantro, for garnish

cook's note: Don't forget to taste. You may want to add an extra spritz of lime juice or a pinch of salt.

Position a rack in the middle of the oven and preheat to 425°F. Line a rimmed baking sheet with parchment paper.

Put the cauliflower, 2 tablespoons of the olive oil, ¼ teaspoon of the turmeric, ½ teaspoon salt, and the pepper in a large bowl and toss until the cauliflower is evenly coated. Transfer to the prepared baking sheet and spread in an even layer. Bake for 20 to 25 minutes, or until golden and tender.

Meanwhile, heat the remaining tablespoon of olive oil in a soup pot over medium heat, then add the onion, a pinch of salt, and the remaining ¼ teaspoon turmeric and sauté until translucent, about 3 minutes. Add the garlic, carrots, celery, and ½ teaspoon salt and sauté until the vegetables begin to turn golden, about 10 minutes. Add the chili paste and stir until the vegetables are coated. Pour in ½ cup of the broth to deglaze the pot, stirring to loosen any bits stuck to the bottom, and cook until the liquid is reduced by half.

Pour one-third of the remaining broth into a blender, add the ginger and one-third of the sautéed vegetables and cauliflower, and blend until smooth, adding more broth as needed. Transfer to a soup pot over low heat and repeat the process two more times. Stir in ¼ teaspoon salt and the lime juice. Serve garnished with the cilantro, or store in an airtight container in the refrigerator for up to 5 days or in the freezer for up to 3 months.

kale soup with coconut and lime

Talk about counterbalancing tastes: here the überhealthy kale and coconut milk are a magical pairing, with the sweetness of the coconut neutralizing the natural bitterness of the kale. The ginger and lime are like Fourth of July sparklers on top of the flavor profile. The soup is purposely a bit thin, and many people enjoy it as a broth in a cup or take it to go in a thermos. If you want to give it a little heft, try adding glass noodles or shredded sweet potato.

2 tablespoons extra-virgin olive oil or coconut oil

2 cloves garlic, minced

2 tablespoons minced fresh ginger

2 bunches kale, stemmed and cut into bite-size pieces

Sea salt

6 cups Thai Coconut Broth (page 36)

1½ tablespoons freshly squeezed lime juice

2½ teaspoons dark maple syrup

1 tablespoon finely chopped fresh Thai basil, for garnish (optional)

Heat the oil in a soup pot over medium-high heat, then add the garlic and ginger, stir, and cook for about 1 minute. Add the kale and ¼ teaspoon sea salt and sauté for 3 minutes, or just until emerald green. Add the broth and cook until the kale is tender, about 3 minutes. Remove from the heat.

Pour 2 cups of the broth into a blender, add one-third of the kale mixture, and blend until smooth. Transfer to a soup pot over low heat, and repeat the process two more times. Stir in the lime juice, maple syrup and ½ teaspoon sea salt. Serve garnished with the basil, or store in an airtight container in the refrigerator for up to 5 days or in the freezer for up to 3 months.

ruby red beet soup

makes 6 servings | prep time: 15 minutes | cook time: 40 minutes

Sometimes the colors that nature comes up with blow me away. Take the ruby red beets and red cabbage in this soup; they're as brilliant as the dahlias that grow in my backyard. So, too, is their taste, and when combined with sautéed onion, fennel, and celery, plus cumin, coriander, and caraway, the result is simply luscious.

3 tablespoons extra-virgin olive oil

1 yellow onion, diced

1 fennel bulb, diced

2 stalks celery, diced

Sea salt

1 teaspoon ground cumin

1 teaspoon ground coriander

1 teaspoon caraway seeds

Pinch of red pepper flakes

6 cups Nourishing Bone Broth (page 41), Pastured Beef Bone Broth (page 43), or Magic Mineral Broth (page 35)

8 ounces red cabbage, chopped

3 beets, peeled and diced

2 tablespoons full-fat plain yogurt, for garnish

2 tablespoons chopped fresh dill, for garnish

cook's note: This is a wonderful soup that can be served hot or cold. If it's been sitting in the refrigerator, give it a taste. You may want to perk it up with a spritz of lemon or orange juice.

Heat the olive oil in a soup pot over medium heat, then add the onion, fennel, celery, and ½ teaspoon salt and sauté until golden, about 6 minutes. Add the cumin, coriander, caraway seeds, and red pepper flakes and stir until well combined. Pour in ½ cup of the broth to deglaze the pot, stirring to loosen any bits stuck to the bottom, and cook until the liquid is reduced by half. Add the cabbage and ¼ teaspoon salt and stir. Add the beets and another ¼ teaspoon salt, stir, and cook for about 1 minute. Add the remaining 5½ cups of broth and ½ teaspoon salt. Bring to a boil, then cover and simmer until the beets are tender, about 25 to 30 minutes.

In a blender, puree the soup in batches until very smooth, each time adding the cooking liquid first and then the vegetables. Pour the soup back into the pot and heat gently. Taste; you may want to add a pinch more salt. Serve garnished with the yogurt and dill, or store in an airtight container in the refrigerator for up to 5 days or in the freezer for up to 3 months.

sweet pea and mint soup

makes 6 servings | prep time: 10 minutes | cook time: 15 minutes

This is my riff on a French classic, minus the cream. Sweet peas and mint naturally complement each other with their delightfully delicate, fresh flavors. I amplify the pea's taste—and nutritional content—by adding pea shoots to the sauté. As for texture, the sautéed buttery Bibb lettuce counterbalances the mealiness of the peas, making for a smooth consistency.

2 tablespoons extra-virgin olive oil

1 large leek, white part only, rinsed and chopped

Sea salt

¼ teaspoon freshly ground black pepper

1 (10-ounce) package frozen sweet peas, defrosted, or 3 cups freshly shelled peas

1 small head Bibb lettuce, torn into pieces

1 cup pea sprouts

2 tablespoons coarsely chopped fresh mint, plus more for garnish

6 cups Old-Fashioned Chicken Stock (page 39) or Magic Mineral Broth (page 35)

1 tablespoon freshly squeezed lemon juice, plus more if needed

6 tablespoons full-fat plain yogurt, for garnish

Peashoots, for garnish (optional)

Heat the olive oil in a soup pot over medium heat, then add the leek, a pinch of salt, and the pepper and sauté until translucent, about 5 minutes. Stir in the peas and the lettuce and another pinch of salt. Pour in ½ cup of the stock to deglaze the pot, stirring to loosen any bits stuck to the bottom, and cook until the liquid is reduced by half. Remove from the heat.

Pour one-third of the remaining stock into a blender, add one-third of the vegetable mixture, one-third of the pea sprouts, and the mint. Blend until smooth. Transfer to a soup pot over low heat. Divide the remaining stock in half and repeat the process two more times. Stir in the lemon juice and ½ teaspoon salt. Taste; you may want to add an additional squeeze of lemon and a couple of pinches of salt. Serve garnished with the yogurt, peashoots, and a bit of mint, or store in an airtight container in the refrigerator for up to 5 days or in the freezer for up to 3 months.

roasted curry sweet potato soup

makes 6 servings | prep time: 15 minutes | cook time: 25 minutes

You might be surprised to find out that curry isn't one spice, but rather an amalgam of six to twelve spices, which ratchets up both the flavor and the anti-inflammatory power. In this soup, the spices all do a lazy backstroke in the pot with the orange-fleshed sweet potatoes, which are rich in magnesium, the antistress mineral. One sip of this and you're on your way to relaxation; one cup and you'll be ready for a hammock.

3 pounds orange-fleshed sweet potatoes, diced

3 tablespoons extra-virgin olive oil

Sea salt

1 tablespoon curry powder

½ teaspoon ground turmeric

½ teaspoon freshly ground black pepper

6 to 8 cups Magic Mineral Broth (page 35), plus more if needed

1 teaspoon freshly squeezed lime or lemon juice

Preheat the oven to 400°F. Line a baking sheet with parchment paper.

In a large bowl, toss the sweet potatoes with the olive oil, 1 teaspoon salt, and the curry powder, turmeric, and pepper until evenly coated. Spread the sweet potatoes in a single layer on the prepared pan and roast for 20 minutes, or until tender.

Pour one-third of the broth into a blender, add one-third of the sweet potatoes, and blend until smooth, adding more liquid as needed. Transfer to a soup pot over low heat and repeat the process two more times.

Stir in the lime juice, any remaining broth, and ¼ teaspoon salt. Store in an airtight container in the refrigerator for up to 5 days or in the freezer for up to 3 months.

summer zucchini soup with basil

makes 6 servings | prep time: 15 minutes | cook time: 15 minutes

When summertime hits, zucchini is in practically every stall at the farmers' market. Getting creative with zucchini is a must, because left to its own devices (raw), it can get a little bossy at times. I like to make zucchini sweat in the pot to release its natural sweetness. Blending in the basil and baby spinach creates a soup that's a stunning shade of green.

2 tablespoons extra-virgin olive oil

1 yellow onion, diced

Sea salt

2 cloves garlic, chopped

3½ pounds zucchini, quartered lengthwise, then cut crosswise into ½-inch pieces

¼ teaspoon red pepper flakes or freshly ground black pepper

6 cups Old-Fashioned Chicken Stock (page 39) or Magic Mineral Broth (page 35)

2 cups tightly packed baby spinach

½ cup loosely packed fresh basil leaves

1 tablespoon freshly squeezed lemon juice, plus more if needed

¼ cup Heirloom Tomato Salsa, (page 132), for garnish

Heat the olive oil in a soup pot over medium heat, then add the onion and a pinch of salt and sauté until golden, about 6 minutes. Add the garlic, zucchini, red pepper flakes, and ¼ teaspoon salt and sauté for 4 minutes. Pour in ½ cup of the stock to deglaze the pot, stirring to loosen any bits stuck to the bottom, and cook until the liquid is reduced by half. Remove from the heat.

Pour one-third of the remaining stock into a blender, add one-third of the zucchini sauté, spinach, and basil, and blend until smooth. Transfer to a soup pot over low heat, and repeat the process two more times. Stir in the lemon juice and ½ teaspoon salt. Taste; you may want to add an additional squeeze of lemon and a couple of pinches of salt. Serve garnished with the salsa, or store in an airtight container in the refrigerator for up to 5 days or in the freezer for up to 3 months.

roasted heirloom tomato soup

makes 6 servings | prep time: 15 minutes | cook time: 30 minutes

I always laugh when I hear people raving about tomato soup and grilled cheese sandwiches. Of course they love it—it's just pizza deconstructed! My favorite way to make tomato soup is to head to the farmers' market and gather all the bruised heirloom tomatoes I can find; you can get a lot for pennies on the dollar, and you don't need pristine tomatoes for this recipe. I roast the tomatoes with garlic, olive oil, and salt, then add just a hint of dark maple syrup to the soup to balance out the tomatoes' natural acidity.

4 pounds yellow heirloom tomatoes, halved

4 cloves garlic, peeled

2 tablespoons extra-virgin olive oil

Sea salt

1 cup loosely packed fresh basil leaves

1 tablespoon dark maple syrup

6 tablespoons Many Herb Drizzle (page 127), for garnish

Endive, for serving (optional)

Preheat the oven to 400°F. Line a rimmed baking sheet with parchment paper.

Put the tomatoes and garlic in a bowl and gently toss with the olive oil and 1 teaspoon salt. Arrange the tomatoes, cut side down, in a single layer on the prepared baking sheet, along with the garlic. Roast for 20 to 25 minutes, or until the tomato skins are just golden and the juices are bubbling. Remove from the oven, cool, and then lift off the skins.

Pick up the parchment paper by the corners and pour the tomatoes, garlic, and their juices into a blender. Blend on high speed for at least 1 minute, until smooth and creamy. Add the basil and pulse a few times, until the basil is shredded and combined.

Pour the mixture into a soup pot, heat gently, and then stir in the maple syrup and ½ teaspoon salt. This soup can be eaten at room temperature, chilled, or warmed. Serve with the drizzle and endive, or store in an airtight container in the refrigerator for up to 5 days or in the freezer for up to 3 months.

escarole soup

Escarole has a somewhat bitter, spicy taste, like its other chicory cousins, and packs a nutritional punch that aids in digestion and detoxification. Here escarole is paired with buttery Bibb lettuce, making this soup anything but bitter. In fact, it's light as a feather and a perfect soup for spring and summer, which is escarole's peak season. It comes together quickly as well; if you have broth on hand you can make the soup, including prep and cooking, in less than half an hour.

2 tablespoons extra-virgin olive oil

1 large leek, white part only, rinsed and diced

Sea salt

3 cloves garlic, minced

1 head escarole, white and green parts separated, rinsed, and chopped

¼ teaspoon freshly ground black pepper

4 cups Chicken Magic Mineral Broth (page 38)

1 head Bibb lettuce, torn into pieces

2 tablespoons chopped fresh flat-leaf parsley

2 teaspoons freshly squeezed lemon juice, plus more if needed

1 teaspoon lemon zest

Heat the olive oil in a soup pot over medium heat, then add leek and a pinch of salt and sauté until very tender, about 8 minutes. Add the garlic and sauté for another 30 seconds, then stir in the white parts of the escarole, ½ teaspoon salt, and the pepper. Pour in ½ cup of the broth to deglaze the pot, stirring to loosen any bits stuck to the bottom, and cook until the liquid is reduced by half.

Stir in the green parts of the escarole and the remaining 3½ cups of broth. Bring to a low boil, then stir in the lettuce and remove from the heat.

Stir in the parsley and blend in batches until very smooth. Return the soup to the pot and stir in the lemon juice and zest. Gently heat the soup before serving. Taste; you may want to add another pinch of salt or squeeze of lemon. Store in an airtight container in the refrigerator for up to 5 days or in the freezer for up to 3 months.

spiced butternut squash soup with cardamom and ginger

makes 6 servings | prep time: 10 minutes | cook time: 35 minutes

Today's soup is brought to you by the color orange and the letter "A," as in vitamin A. If you're craving something naturally sweet, this soup works wonders. The squash, carrots, orange zest, and cardamom sing a sweet song indeed, and the nutrients in this dish provide their own high note. Vitamin A is great at maintaining the integrity of the immune system, while the spices—including ginger, cumin, and coriander—are outstanding anti-inflammatories.

2 tablespoons extra-virgin olive oil

Sea salt

1 teaspoon ground cumin

½ teaspoon ground coriander

¼ teaspoon ground cardamom

4 carrots, peeled and sliced 1 inch thick

1 pound butternut squash, peeled, seeded, and cut into 1-inch cubes (see Cook's Note on page 47)

6 cups Magic Mineral Broth (page 35), plus more if needed

¼ teaspoon freshly ground black pepper

1 teaspoon grated fresh ginger

¼ teaspoon orange zest

2 tablespoon freshly squeezed orange juice

1 tablespoon freshly squeezed lemon juice, plus more if needed

Preheat the oven to 400°F. Line a baking sheet with parchment paper.

In a large bowl combine the olive oil, ¼ teaspoon salt, and the cumin, coriander, and cardamom; stir until well combined. Add the carrots and butternut squash and toss until evenly coated. Spread the vegetables in a single layer on the prepared baking sheet and roast for 30 minutes, or until tender.

Pour one-third of the broth into a blender. Add the pepper, ginger, orange zest, and one-third of the roasted vegetables and blend until smooth, adding more liquid as needed. Transfer to a soup pot over low heat and repeat the process two more times. Stir in ¼ teaspoon salt and the orange juice and lemon juice. Taste; you may want to add another spritz of lemon juice or a pinch of salt. Store in an airtight container in the refrigerator for up to 5 days or in the freezer for up to 3 months.

celeriac soup with crispy shiitake mushrooms

makes 6 servings | prep time: 15 minutes | cook time: 40 minutes

Sometimes I wonder who was the first brave soul to tear apart a celery root and cook with it. To look at a celery root (or celeriac) and see promise is the definition of an optimist; it's knobby, hairy covering gives no hint of the delicacy within, but it's there, all the same. Sautéed with garlic, leek, and fennel, it yields a very pleasant taste—to take this soup right over the top.

3 tablespoons extra-virgin olive oil

1 large leek, white part only, rinsed and diced

2 stalks celery, diced

Sea salt

2 cloves garlic, minced

2 pounds celery root (celeriac), peeled and diced

1 fennel bulb, diced

6 cups Magic Mineral Broth (page 35), plus more if needed

1 tablespoon freshly squeezed lemon juice

¼ teaspoon dark maple syrup

¼ cup Crispy Shiitake Mushrooms (page 123), for garnish

Heat the olive oil in a soup pot over medium heat, then add the leek, celery, and ¼ teaspoon salt and sauté until the vegetables begin to get tender, about 6 minutes. Stir in the garlic and cook for another 30 seconds, then stir in the celery root, fennel, and another ¼ teaspoon salt. Sauté for about 5 minutes more, stirring often. Pour in ½ cup of the broth to deglaze the pot, stirring to loosen any bits stuck to the bottom, and cook until the liquid is reduced by half.

Add the remaining 5½ cups of broth and another ¼ teaspoon salt. Bring to a boil, then cover and simmer until the vegetables are tender, 20 to 25 minutes.

In a blender, puree the soup in batches until very smooth, each time adding the cooking liquid first and then the vegetables, and adding additional liquid, as needed. Pour the soup back into the pot, heat gently, and stir in the lemon juice. Taste; you may want to add a pinch more salt. Serve garnished with the mushrooms, or store in an airtight container in the refrigerator for up to 5 days or in the freezer for up to 3 months.

traditional
healing soups

Take a map of the world, throw a dart at it, and chances are you'll hit a place that has a hearty, robust soup as part of its traditional cuisine. It doesn't matter whether it's Asia or Europe, India or Mexico, I think we can learn a lot from observing (and tasting!) hearty soups from around the globe. Sure, we can claim good old chicken soup here in the U. S. of A. (indeed, no one made chicken soup like my nana; page 96), but the rest of the globe can still teach us a thing or two about using locally sourced produce, herbs, and spices to create amazingly nutritious and exquisitely mouthwatering fare.

Hearty soups should have *big* taste. That's what you'll find throughout this chapter: soups that are substantial and more like meals in a bowl (I like to call them "cozy bowls"). There are flavor profiles galore. Many you've probably heard of, such as Cuban Black Bean Soup (page 87), Provençal Lentil Soup (page 107), and Hot-and-Sour Shiitake Mushroom Soup (page 90). Others may appear more exotic, such as Indian Mulligatawny (page 95), Japanese Kinpira Gobo (page 91), and Vietnamese Simplest Chicken Pho (page 108). But regardless of whether you've heard of them or not, know that all these soups will leave you with a feeling of being truly nourished and satiated.

What's great is that if you have your broths and stocks already made and stored (see page 12), these traditional soups will come together quickly. Make a few of them and don't be surprised if suddenly you have a reputation for being quite the soup maven.

caramelized fennel and chickpea soup with saffron

makes 6 servings | prep time: 15 minutes | cook time: 35 minutes

The depth of taste in this soup comes from letting the onion and fennel caramelize in the pot without any interference from the carrots. It takes about eight minutes, more or less, and you can tell you're close when the onion starts to stick to the pot and turns from translucent to a golden hue.

2 tablespoons extra-virgin olive oil

2 fennel bulbs, diced small

1 yellow onion, diced small

Sea salt

1 carrot, peeled and diced small

2 cloves garlic, minced

1 teaspoon ground cumin

¼ teaspoon ground coriander

Generous pinch of saffron (20 threads; see Cook's Note)

Pinch of red pepper flakes

6 cups Magic Mineral Broth (page 35) or Chicken Magic Mineral Broth (page 38)

1 tablespoon plus 1 teaspoon freshly squeezed lemon juice, plus more if needed

4 cups cooked chickpeas, or 2 (15-ounce) cans of chickpeas, rinsed

¼ teaspoon orange zest

1 teaspoon lemon zest

2 tablespoons chopped fresh flat-leaf parsley, for garnish

1 tablespoon chopped fresh mint, for garnish

cook's note: When I say twenty threads of saffron (a generous pinch) and no more, best to pay heed. Saffron is flavorful in just the right amount, but too much can quickly overpower both the soup and your taste buds.

Heat the olive oil in a soup pot over medium heat, then add the fennel, onion, and a pinch of salt and sauté until golden, about 8 minutes. Add the carrot and sauté another 3 minutes. Stir in the garlic and cook for 30 seconds. Add the cumin, coriander, saffron, red pepper flakes, and ½ teaspoon salt and stir for another 30 seconds, or until fragrant. Pour in ½ cup of the broth to deglaze the pot, stirring to loosen any bits stuck to the bottom, and cook until the liquid is reduced by half.

Add 1 tablespoon of the lemon juice and ½ teaspoon salt to the chickpeas and stir, then add to the pot. Add the remaining 5½ cups of broth, increase the heat to medium-high, and bring to a boil. Decrease the heat to medium, cover, and simmer for 15 minutes.

Ladle 4 cups of the soup into a blender and process for 1 minute, or until velvety smooth. Stir the blended mixture back into the soup and cook over low heat just until heated through.

Stir in the orange zest, lemon zest, and remaining 1 teaspoon of lemon juice. Taste; you may want to add a pinch of salt or another squeeze of lemon. Serve garnished with the cilantro and mint, or store in an airtight container in the refrigerator for up to 5 days or in the freezer for up to 3 months.

caramelized onion soup with pastured beef bone broth

makes 6 servings | prep time: 20 minutes | cook time: 40 minutes

Onion soup is considered French (at least when it's smothered in croutons and Gruyère cheese), but in fact it goes back to the days of the Romans. This soup is all about having patience with the onions. I'll admit, the hardest thing as a soup-maker is knowing when to put the spoon down, but here you need to give the onions time, 20 to 25 minutes, without stirring to let them wilt, turn a golden hue, and release all their natural sugars. If you can do that, your patience will be well rewarded with a delectable, rich, sweet onion soup.

3 tablespoons extra-virgin olive oil

3 pounds red onions, halved and sliced ½ inch thick

Sea salt

¼ teaspoon dried thyme, or 1 teaspoon chopped fresh thyme

1 teaspoon Dijon mustard

6 cups Pastured Beef Bone Broth (page 43), Nourishing Bone Broth (page 41), or Magic Mineral Broth (page 35)

Pinch of freshly grated nutmeg

1 teaspoon freshly squeezed lemon juice, plus more if needed

2 teaspoons dark maple syrup

2 tablespoons finely chopped fresh flat-leaf parsley, for garnish

In a large, straight-sided sauté pan or large soup pot, heat the olive oil over medium heat. Add the onions and ½ teaspoon salt and stir. Decrease the heat to medium-low. Cook without stirring for about 25 minutes, or until the onions have turned a deep golden brown. Stir in the thyme and mustard until well combined. Pour in ½ cup of the broth to deglaze the pot, stirring to loosen any bits stuck to the bottom, and cook until the liquid is reduced by half.

Add the remaining 5½ cups of broth, ½ teaspoon salt, and the nutmeg. Increase the heat to high and bring to a boil. Decrease the heat to low, cover, and simmer for 10 more minutes. Stir in the lemon juice and the maple syrup and taste; you may want to add a spritz of lemon juice or a pinch or two of salt. Serve garnished with the parsley, or store in an airtight container in the refrigerator for up to 5 days or in the freezer for up to 3 months.

congee

makes 6 servings | prep time: 5 minutes | cook time: 2 hours

Congee is an ancient Chinese porridge, dating back more than two thousand years. When Americans think about porridge, oatmeal comes to mind. This broth-based congee is thinner, but it's stimulating and satisfying. Its whole grain brown rice base is perfect for jump-starting digestion (some people even eat it for breakfast), and it's a nice canvas for adding taste-enhancers ranging from scallions to cinnamon.

1 cup soaked short-grain brown rice (see Cook's Notes)

8 cups Old-Fashioned Chicken Stock (page 39), plus more if needed

1 tablespoon minced fresh ginger

¾ teaspoon sea salt

1 tablespoon tamari

¼ teaspoon freshly squeezed lemon juice

Toasted sesame oil, minced scallion, or chopped fresh cilantro, for garnish (optional)

In a heavy soup pot over high heat, combine the soaked rice, stock, ginger, and salt. Bring to a boil, then decrease the heat to low and cook, covered, until a soft porridge-like consistency is achieved, about 2 hours. Add more stock or water if it gets too thick. Mix in the tamari and lemon juice. Serve garnished with the sesame oil, or store in an airtight container in the refrigerator for up to 5 days or in the freezer for up to 3 months.

cook's notes: To soak the rice, put 1 cup of rice in a large bowl and cover with cool water and the juice of ½ lemon. Soak for 8 hours or overnight, then drain well before cooking. This will make its nutrients more available and decrease the cooking time. If you don't have time to soak the rice, add an extra cup of stock and cook for an additional 15 minutes.

Congee tastes even better the next day. Add ½ to 1 cup of stock to reheat in a heavy pot over medium-low heat.

cuban black bean soup

makes 6 servings | prep time: 15 minutes | cook time: 25 minutes

What makes this soup so delicious is that after it cooks, I take half of it and blend it (if you don't want to ladle it out, use an immersion blender in the pot). This adds a level of creaminess to the soup's natural chunkiness. Here I top it with Polenta Croutons for a third mouthfeel: crunchy.

2 tablespoons extra-virgin olive oil

1 yellow onion, diced

Sea salt

1 red bell pepper, finely diced

1 small jalapeño pepper, seeded and finely diced

2 cloves garlic, minced

1½ teaspoons dried oregano

1 teaspoon ground cumin

¼ teaspoon ground cinnamon

6 cups Magic Mineral Broth (page 35)

4 cups cooked black beans, or 2 (15-ounce) cans, rinsed

4 teaspoons freshly squeezed lime juice, plus more if needed

½ teaspoon lime zest

1 teaspoon dark maple syrup (optional)

2 tablespoons chopped fresh cilantro, for garnish

Polenta Croutons (page 137), for garnish

Heat the olive oil in a soup pot over medium heat, then add the onion and a pinch of salt and sauté until the onion is translucent, about 6 minutes. Add the bell pepper, jalapeño, garlic, oregano, cumin, cinnamon, and ¼ teaspoon salt and sauté for 1 minute. Pour in ½ cup of the broth to deglaze the pot, stirring to loosen any bits stuck to the bottom, and cook until the liquid is reduced by half.

Spritz the black beans with 2 teaspoons of the lime juice, add a pinch of salt, stir, then add to the pot. Add the remaining 5½ cups of broth. Increase the heat to medium-high. Bring to a boil, then decrease the heat to medium, cover, and simmer for 15 minutes.

Ladle 3 cups of the soup into a blender and process for 1 minute, or until velvety smooth. Stir the blended mixture back into the soup and cook over low heat just until heated through. Stir in the lime zest, the remaining 2 teaspoons of lime juice, and ½ teaspoon salt. Taste; you may want to add another pinch of salt, a squeeze of lime, or 1 teaspoon of maple syrup. Serve garnished with the cilantro and croutons, or store in an airtight container in the refrigerator for up to 5 days or in the freezer for up to 3 months.

kitchari

makes 6 servings | prep time: 15 minutes | cook time: 1 hour

Head to India and Pakistan, where they've been practicing Ayurvedic medicine for 5,000 years, for detoxing and improving memory. Kitchari, which means "mixture," is a thousand-year-old staple, and its really quite simple, traditionally being made with basmati rice, mung beans, and ghee. I've kicked it up quite a bit, adding onion, ginger, cauliflower, coriander, turmeric, and cumin. The result is the spice mixture of a dal combined with kitchari's texture.

2 tablespoons ghee, extra-virgin olive oil, or coconut oil

1 onion, diced

2 tablespoons minced fresh ginger

2 tablespoons minced fresh turmeric

1 teaspoon ground cumin

½ teaspoon ground turmeric

½ teaspoon ground coriander

1¼ teaspoons sea salt, plus more if needed

½ cup split mung beans, rinsed and soaked (see Cook's Notes)

½ cup brown basmati rice, rinsed and soaked (see Cook's Notes)

5 to 6 cups Magic Mineral Broth (page 35)

1 head cauliflower, chopped into florets

2 carrots, peeled and diced

1 teaspoon freshly squeezed lemon juice, plus more if needed

2 tablespoons minced fresh cilantro, for garnish

Heat the ghee in a heavy-bottomed pot over medium heat, then add the onion and sauté for about 4 minutes, or just until golden. Stir in the ginger, fresh turmeric, cumin, ground turmeric, coriander, and salt and sauté for about 1 minute. Add the beans and rice and stir to coat. Add 5 cups of the broth and bring to a boil. Decrease the heat to low and simmer, covered, for about 20 minutes, or until the rice begins to soften. Stir in the cauliflower and carrots and continue to cook until very tender and soft, another 20 minutes. Add another cup of broth if it becomes too thick. Stir in the lemon juice. Taste; it may need another spritz of lemon juice or another pinch of salt. Serve garnished with the cilantro, or store in an airtight container in the refrigerator for up to 5 days or in the freezer for up to 3 months.

cook's notes: To soak the beans and rice, put them in a large bowl and add water to cover by 3 inches. Cover with a towel and soak for 8 hours or overnight. Drain well just before cooking.

Kitchari is even better the next day; however, it will absorb most of the liquid, so you may need to add some broth or water to thin it out before reheating in a soup pot over medium-low heat.

hot-and-sour shiitake mushroom soup

makes 4 servings | prep time: 20 minutes | cook time: 20 minutes

Back in my go-go thirties (where has the time gone?), I used to live on hot-and-sour soup from my favorite Baltimore Chinese carryout. Truth is, I always felt I could do them one better, and this soup proves that out. There's no cornstarch thickener in my version (nor in traditional Chinese hot-and-sour soup). Plus, here I include shiitake mushrooms, which have great anti-inflammatory benefits. The rest is carrot, scallions, ginger, Napa cabbage, tamari, rice wine vinegar, red pepper flakes, and, for protein, egg. Makes me want to open my own carryout.

2 tablespoons extra-virgin olive oil

1 carrot, peeled and diced

1 pound fresh shiitake mushrooms, sliced

4 scallions, sliced, with the green parts set aside

Sea salt

1 tablespoon minced fresh ginger

⅛ teaspoon red pepper flakes

1 head Napa cabbage, chopped (about 3 cups)

3 tablespoons tamari

6 cups Magic Mineral Broth (page 35)

2 tablespoons rice wine vinegar

1 egg, lightly beaten

2 tablespoons freshly squeezed lime juice

Heat the olive oil in a soup pot over medium heat, then add the carrot, mushrooms, scallions, and a pinch of salt and sauté until soft, about 8 minutes. Add the ginger and red pepper flakes and sauté for about 30 seconds. Add the cabbage and another pinch of salt and sauté until the cabbage is wilted, about 3 minutes. Stir in the tamari and ½ cup of the broth to deglaze the pot, stirring to loosen any bits stuck to the bottom, and cook until the liquid is reduced by half.

Add the remaining 5½ cups broth and the vinegar and bring to a boil. Decrease the heat to a low simmer, drizzle in the egg through a slotted spoon, and cook for 1 minute more. Stir in the lime juice. Serve garnished with the scallion tops, or store in an airtight container in the refrigerator for up to 5 days or in the freezer for up to 3 months.

kinpira gobo

makes 6 servings | prep time: 15 minutes | cook time: 30 minutes

Kinpira gobo is Japanese for "braised burdock root." Burdock root mimics the satisfying taste of mushrooms, is fiber rich, and soaks up whatever flavors are in its neighborhood. It's a staple in macrobiotic cooking, but here I really amp up the nutrition and tang by sautéing the burdock with onion, carrots, ginger, red pepper flakes, mirin, and tamari. This soup makes you feel like you're drawing sustenance from Mother Earth. It's a lovely, rooted sensation, perfect for when you could use a little grounding.

2 tablespoons sesame oil

1 yellow onion, sliced

Sea salt

2 carrots, peeled and cut into thin matchsticks

1 (6-inch) piece burdock root, cut into thin matchsticks

1 tablespoon minced fresh ginger

⅛ teaspoon red pepper flakes

4 cups Magic Mineral Broth (page 35) or Immune Broth (page 40), plus more if needed

2 tablespoons low-sodium tamari

1 tablespoon mirin

½ teaspoon rice vinegar

3 scallions, white and green parts, sliced, for garnish

Heat the sesame oil in a soup pot over medium heat, then add the onion and a generous pinch of salt and cook, partially covered, for 12 minutes, stirring occasionally, until the onion begins to brown around the edges. Add the carrots, burdock, ginger, red pepper flakes, and another generous pinch of salt and cook, stirring occasionally for 10 minutes, or until the carrots are tender. Add 2 tablespoons of the broth if the mixture gets too dry. Stir in the tamari, mirin, and ½ cup of the broth to deglaze the pot, stirring to loosen any bits stuck to the bottom, and cook until the liquid is reduced by half. Add the remaining 3½ cups of broth. Increase the heat to medium-high until the soup simmers, then stir in the vinegar and remove from the heat. Serve garnished with the scallions or store in an airtight container in the refrigerator for up to 5 days or in the freezer for up to 3 months.

latin american chicken soup with greens

makes 6 servings | prep time: 15 minutes | cook time: 25 minutes

There's a misconception that in Mexican cooking the only greens used are herbs, such as cilantro. In fact, gathering and consuming greens goes back centuries in Mexico. Swiss chard is a hugely popular Mexican green, and it's the base green in this soup. This is like tortilla soup without the tortilla. It's refreshing and invigorating, and after eating it, you'll never think of Mexican food quite the same way again.

2 tablespoons extra-virgin olive oil

1 yellow onion, diced small

Sea salt

2 carrots, peeled and diced

2 stalks celery, diced

1 red bell pepper, diced

1 small jalapeño pepper, seeded and diced

2 cloves garlic, chopped

½ teaspoon ground cumin

¼ teaspoon dried oregano

1 (14.5-ounce) can diced tomatoes

6 cups Old-Fashioned Chicken Stock (page 39) or Chicken Magic Mineral Broth (page 38)

½ bunch Swiss chard, stemmed and thinly sliced

1 cup cooked and thinly sliced cooked chicken (see Cook's Note)

2 tablespoons freshly squeezed lime juice

2 tablespoons chopped fresh cilantro, for garnish

½ avocado, diced, for garnish

Polenta Croutons (page 137), for garnish (optional)

Heat the olive oil in a soup pot over medium-high heat, then add the onion, ¼ teaspoon salt, carrots, celery, bell peppers, and jalapeño. Sauté the vegetables until they begin to soften, 3 to 5 minutes. Stir in the garlic, cumin, and oregano. Stir in the tomatoes with their juice and ¼ teaspoon salt and cook for 1 minute. Add the stock and bring to a boil. Decrease the heat to low, cover, and simmer for 15 minutes. Stir in the chard and cook until it's just tender, about 1 more minute. Stir in the chicken, lime juice, and ½ teaspoon salt. Serve garnished with the cilantro, avocado, and polenta croutons, or store in an airtight container in the refrigerator for up to 5 days or in the freezer for up to 3 months.

cook's note: If you don't have leftover chicken on hand, you can quickly poach two skinless boneless breasts. The following method produces a delicate flavor by infusing the flavor of the stock liquid into the chicken. Season the breasts with salt and pepper. In a straight-sided skillet, bring 3 cups of stock to a boil over high heat. Add the chicken, cover, and decrease the heat to low. The liquid should be just below the boiling point, with its surface barely quivering. Cook for 15 minutes, then remove the chicken from the poaching liquid and let cool.

herby tuscan bean and vegetable soup

makes 6 servings | prep time: 20 minutes | cook time: 20 minutes

What I love about this soup is how it's filled with the wonderful flavor of fresh veggies and herbs. It's an ode to the zest of Mediterranean cooking. I'm passionate about using herbs in soups. They add a lightness to the overall flavor print, and are chock-full of health benefits.

2 cups cooked cannellini beans, or 1 (15-ounce) can cannellini beans, rinsed

4 teaspoons freshly squeezed lemon juice

Sea salt

2 tablespoons extra-virgin olive oil

1 yellow onion, finely diced

2 cloves garlic, minced

2 large carrots, peeled and finely diced

4 stalks celery, finely chopped

2 teaspoons chopped fresh oregano, or ½ teaspoon dried oregano

¼ teaspoon freshly ground pepper

1 zucchini, finely chopped

1 (14.5-ounce) can diced tomatoes, drained and juice reserved

6 cups Old-Fashioned Chicken Stock (page 39), Magic Mineral Broth (page 35), or Nourishing Bone Broth (page 41)

1 teaspoon lemon zest

2 cups tightly packed baby arugula

3 tablespoons finely chopped fresh flat-leaf parsley

3 tablespoons finely chopped fresh basil (see Variation)

In a bowl, stir together the beans, 2 teaspoons of the lemon juice, and a pinch of salt. Set aside.

In a soup pot, heat the olive oil over medium heat, then add the onion and a pinch of salt and sauté until translucent, about 4 minutes. Add the garlic, carrots, celery, oregano, pepper, and ¼ teaspoon salt, and sauté for 4 minutes more. Pour in the reserved tomato juice and ½ cup of the stock to deglaze the pot, stirring to loosen any bits stuck to the bottom, and cook until the liquid is reduced by half.

Stir in the zucchini, tomatoes, and beans, the remaining 5½ cups of stock, and ¼ teaspoon salt. Bring to a boil over medium heat, then decrease the heat and simmer until the vegetables are tender. Stir the remaining 2 teaspoons of lemon juice and the lemon zest, arugula, parsley, basil, and another ¼ teaspoon salt. Store in an airtight container in the refrigerator for up to 5 days or in the freezer for up to 3 months.

variation: Basil is in season from mid to late summer. In the winter, replace the basil with 1 teaspoon fresh rosemary, 2 teaspoons fresh sage, and 2 tablespoons fresh parsley.

mulligatawny

makes 6 servings | prep time: 15 minutes | cook time: 30 minutes

Indian for "pepper water," mulligatawny was appropriated and popularized by eighteenth-century British colonialists who brought it back to the Empire. It quickly became a taste sensation, spreading as far as Australia. Like dal, there are dozens of mulligatawny variations, most of which use peppers, cream, and curry powder. In my take, the creaminess comes from coconut milk, and the black pepper and curry add a kick to veggies, which include onion, celery, chickpeas, and chard. This is the kind of mulligatawny you'd find while wandering the East End of London, where all the best Indian restaurants reside.

2 tablespoons extra-virgin olive oil, ghee, or coconut oil

1 yellow onion, diced

2 stalks celery, chopped

Sea salt

1 bunch Swiss chard, leaves and stems separated and chopped

4 cloves garlic, chopped

1 tablespoon minced fresh ginger

1½ teaspoons curry powder

½ teaspoon ground turmeric

½ teaspoon ground cumin

¼ teaspoon freshly ground black pepper

1 (14.5-ounce) can diced tomatoes, drained and juice reserved

4 cups Magic Mineral Broth (page 35) or Chicken Magic Mineral Broth (page 38)

1 (15-ounce) can chickpeas, rinsed

Spritz of lime juice, plus more if needed

1 (15-ounce) can coconut milk

Heat the olive oil in a soup pot over medium heat, then add the onion, celery, and a pinch of salt and sauté until golden, about 6 minutes. Add the chard stems and sauté another 3 minutes. Stir in the garlic, ginger, curry powder, turmeric, cumin, and pepper and cook for 30 seconds. Pour in the reserved tomato juice and ¼ cup of the broth to deglaze the pot, stirring to loosen any bits stuck to the bottom, and cook until the liquid is reduced by half.

Spritz the chickpeas with the lime juice, add a pinch of salt, and stir, then add to the pot. Stir in the tomatoes and coconut milk and the remaining 3¾ cups of broth and bring to a boil over medium-high heat. Decrease the heat to medium, cover, and simmer for 10 minutes. Stir in the chard leaves and cook just until wilted, about 2 minutes more. Taste; you may want to add a pinch of salt or a spritz of lime juice. Store in an airtight container in the refrigerator for up to 5 days or in the freezer for up to 3 months.

nana's chicken soup with zucchini noodles

makes 6 servings | prep time: 20 minutes | cook time: 25 minutes

Some things are reflexive. Feeling yucky but hungry? Ninety-nine times out of one hundred, chicken soup fits the bill. Science has shown that chicken soup clears sinuses, but really did we need the PhDs to tell us what grandmothers have known since time immemorial? "Drink this and you'll feel better," was what my nana used to say, and boy was she right. I've honored her recipe here in all ways but one: instead of using old-fashioned egg noodles, I've taken a handheld spiralizer and run a zucchini through it. When you put these zucchini noodles in at the end of the simmering time, they have an al dente texture. It really completes the soup, and it will help you feel right as rain.

2 tablespoons extra-virgin olive oil

1 yellow onion, finely diced

2 large carrots, peeled and cut into rounds

4 stalks celery, sliced into ½-inch chunks

Sea salt

6 cups Old-Fashioned Chicken Stock (page 39)

2 cups cooked and thinly sliced organic chicken (see Cook's Note on page 92)

1 zucchini, peeled and spiralized or cut into thin noodles (see Cook's Note)

1 teaspoon lemon zest

2 teaspoons freshly squeezed lemon juice

2 tablespoons finely chopped fresh flat-leaf parsley or dill, for garnish

Heat the olive oil in a soup pot over medium heat, then add the onion, carrots, celery, and ¼ teaspoon salt and sauté until golden, about 8 minutes. Pour in ½ cup of the stock to deglaze the pot, stirring to loosen any bits stuck to the bottom, and cook until the liquid is reduced by half.

Add the remaining 5½ cups of stock, bring to a boil over medium heat, then decrease the heat and simmer until the vegetables are tender, about 10 minutes. Stir in the chicken, zucchini noodles, lemon zest, and lemon juice and cook for 2 minutes more. Serve garnished with the parsley, or store in an airtight container in the refrigerator for up to 5 days or in the freezer for up to 3 months.

cook's note: Only put in the amount of zucchini noodles you will eat at the time. Letting them sit in the soup and reheating will turn them into mush, just like regular noodles. Refrigerate leftover, uncooked zucchini noodles in a separate airtight container. Add them to the soup when you reheat the leftovers.

salmon coconut chowder

makes 6 servings | prep time: 15 minutes | cook time: 15 minutes

This soup goes to show that if you have broth in the freezer, you can make almost anything. A quick glance showed that I had a stash of Thai Coconut Broth waiting for a dance partner. That turned out to be salmon, as the coconut broth makes an ideal poaching liquid. Poaching is nothing more than gentle cooking in liquid. *Gentle* is the key word: if the broth were at rolling boil, the salmon would fall apart. Instead, by cooking at just below the boiling point (the surface of the water should be barely quivering), the coconut broth infuses its flavors into the fish while cooking it all the way through. The veggies go in at the end so they're tender but not overcooked. It's a lovely chowdah.

1½ pounds wild salmon fillet, pin bones removed, cut into 1-inch cubes

Sea salt

1 tablespoon coconut oil or grapeseed oil

1 yellow onion, diced

2 cloves garlic, minced

1 tablespoon finely chopped fresh ginger

4 cups Thai Coconut Broth (page 36)

1 (15-ounce) can coconut milk

1 small red bell pepper, diced

¼ pound of broccoli, cut into florets

2 tablespoons plus 1 teaspoon freshly squeezed lime juice

¼ teaspoon dark maple syrup

2 scallions, white and green parts, thinly sliced on the diagonal, for garnish

2 tablespoons chopped fresh cilantro, for garnish

Season the salmon with ½ teaspoon salt.

Heat the oil in a soup pot over medium-high heat, then add the onion and a pinch of salt and sauté until translucent, about 3 minutes. Stir in the garlic and ginger and cook for 30 seconds. Add the broth and coconut milk and bring to a gentle boil. Decrease the heat to medium, slide the salmon cubes into the broth, and simmer for 3 minutes. Add the bell pepper and broccoli and cook for 3 minutes more, or until the vegetables are just tender. Stir in the lime juice, maple syrup, and ½ teaspoon salt. Serve garnished with the scallions and cilantro, or store in an airtight container in the refrigerator for up to 3 days or in the freezer for up to 3 months.

smoky split pea soup

makes 6 servings | prep time: 15 minutes | cook time: 1 hour

Split pea was a soup staple in my house growing up. My mom used to add ham hocks to the split peas to create that smoky flavor. My version foregoes the meat and includes smoked paprika to mimic the flavor of the ham. I also blend the soup, which reduces the natural chalkiness of the split peas and creates a velvety texture.

2 tablespoons extra-virgin olive oil, plus more for drizzling

1 yellow onion, finely diced

Sea salt

2 carrots, peeled and finely diced

2 stalks celery, finely diced

¼ teaspoon dried thyme

¼ teaspoon smoked paprika

Freshly ground black pepper

2 cloves garlic, minced

2 cups dried green split peas, rinsed well

8 cups Magic Mineral Broth (page 35)

2 teaspoons freshly squeezed lemon juice, plus more if needed

Heat the olive oil in a soup pot over medium heat, then add the onion and a pinch of salt and sauté until golden, about 8 minutes. Add the carrots, celery, thyme, paprika, ¼ teaspoon salt, and ⅛ teaspoon pepper and sauté for about 8 minutes, or just until golden. Stir in the garlic and split peas, then pour in ½ cup of the broth, stirring to deglaze the pot, and cook until the liquid is reduced by half.

Add the remaining 7½ cups of broth, increase the heat to high, and bring to a boil. Decrease the heat to low and simmer, stirring occasionally, until the split peas are tender, about 40 minutes.

Ladle 2 cups of the soup into a blender and process for 1 minute, until velvety smooth. Stir the blended mixture back into to the soup and cook just until heated through. Stir in the lemon juice, ¼ teaspoon salt, and a few grinds of pepper. Taste; you may want to add a spritz of lemon juice or a pinch of salt. Serve garnished with a drizzle of olive oil, or store in an airtight container in the refrigerator for up to 5 days or in the freezer for up to 3 months.

african sweet potato and peanut soup

makes 6 servings | prep time: 15 minutes | cook time: 30 minutes

At first glance the main ingredients in this recipe may seem like a totally random (and somewhat odd) combo, but it's actually a classic Ethiopian soup. It will have your taste buds rockin' and rollin' thanks to berbere, an Ethiopian spice mix. Traditional berbere has about thirteen(!) spices; I shortened that down to a more manageable number of spices, but you'll still get that spicy-sweet-hot tension. The sweet potato here is like the grand marshal of the parade, pulling all those spices and veggies into cohesion to provide a sensational experience.

2 tablespoons extra-virgin olive oil

1 yellow onion, diced

Sea salt

1 small red bell pepper, diced

2 cloves garlic, minced

2 teaspoons finely grated fresh ginger

½ teaspoon ground allspice

½ teaspoon ground cinnamon

½ teaspoon sweet paprika

⅛ teaspoon cayenne pepper

1 (14.5-ounce) can diced tomatoes

3 tablespoons smooth peanut butter

6 cups Magic Mineral Broth (page 35)

2 pounds garnet yams (sweet potatoes), peeled and cut into ½-inch cubes

1 tablespoon freshly squeeezed lime juice, plus more if needed

1 small bunch fresh cilantro, chopped, for garnish

½ cup chopped peanuts, for garnish

Heat the olive oil in a large soup pot over medium-high heat, then add the onion and a pinch of salt and sauté until translucent, about 6 minutes. Add the bell pepper, garlic, ginger, allspice, cinnamon, paprika, and cayenne and sauté for 1 minute more. Stir in the tomatoes with their juice and the peanut butter. Pour in ½ cup of the broth to deglaze the pot, stirring to loosen any bits stuck to the bottom, and cook until the liquid is reduced by half.

Stir in the sweet potatoes, ½ teaspoon sea salt, and the remaining 5½ cups of broth. Bring to a boil, then decrease the heat to medium, cover, and simmer for 15 minutes, or until the sweet potatoes are tender.

Ladle 3 cups of the soup into a blender and process for 1 minute, or until velvety smooth. Stir the blended mixture back into the soup and cook over low heat just until heated through. Stir in the lime juice. Taste; you may want to add a generous pinch of salt or a bit more lime juice. Serve garnished with the cilantro and peanuts, or store in an airtight container in the refrigerator for up to 5 days or in the freezer for up to 3 months.

shiro miso soup with daikon noodles

makes 6 servings | prep time: 10 minutes | cook time: 15 minutes

Miso, which is made by fermenting soybeans, often in combination with various grains, is one of the world's healthiest foods and dates back to seventh-century Japan. There are many kinds of miso, differentiated by color, which in turn is dependent upon fermentation time. Shiro miso is white or yellow and has a lighter flavor and lower salt content than reddish or dark brown miso. Shiro miso also utilizes rice, rather than barley, making it gluten-free. It's not unusual for the Japanese to start their day with a bowl of miso soup, and given their long-lived nature, it's hard to argue with that practice.

2 tablespoons extra-virgin olive oil

1 carrot, diced small

12 fresh shiitake mushrooms, sliced

4 scallions, thinly sliced, with the dark green parts set aside

6 cups Magic Mineral Broth (page 35)

1 tablespoon white miso

½ teaspoon freshly squeezed lime juice or rice vinegar

2 cups lightly packed baby spinach

1 (10-inch) daikon, peeled and spiralized or cut into noodles

Heat the olive oil in a soup pot over medium heat, then add the carrot and shiitakes and sauté until they just begin to turn brown, about 3 minutes. Add the white and light green parts of the scallions and a pinch of salt and sauté until the carrot is just tender, about 8 minutes. Add 5½ cups of the broth and bring to a low simmer. Dissolve the miso in the remaining ½ cup broth, then stir it into the soup, along with the lime juice. Stir in the spinach and remove from heat.

Divide the daikon noodles among 4 bowls and ladle in the hot broth. Garnish each bowl with the scallion tops and serve immediately, or store in an airtight container in the refrigerator for up to 5 days or in the freezer for up to 3 months.

tom yum gai

makes 6 servings | prep time: 15 minutes | cook time: 20 minutes

If you were to translate the name of this soup literally from the Thai, it works out to "boiled spicy and sour salad with chicken." Trust me, it tastes out-of-this-world good. My version of this Thai and Vietnamese staple includes lemongrass, kaffir lime leaves (the bay leaf of Thailand), and coconut milk in the broth, as well as ginger and chili paste. This is a hearty soup that will leave you feeling as though you've had a meal. Nutritionally, it's full of anti-inflammatory ingredients, most notably the ginger and coconut milk.

1 teaspoon Thai red chili paste

1 tablespoon coconut palm sugar

1 teaspoon grated fresh ginger

4 cups Thai Coconut Broth (page 36)

1 tablespoon fish sauce, plus more if needed

2 tablespoons freshly squeezed lime juice, plus more if needed

½ yellow onion, thinly sliced

12 fresh shiitake mushrooms, thinly sliced

2 cups cooked and shredded organic chicken (see Cook's Note on page 92), peeled and deveined shrimp, or cubed tofu

2 tablespoons chopped fresh cilantro, for garnish

In a soup pot over medium heat, toast the chili paste, sugar, and ginger for 1 minute, stirring to combine. Add the broth, fish sauce, and lime juice and bring to a boil, then cover and simmer for 5 minutes. Stir in the onion, mushrooms, and chicken, cover, and cook for 10 minutes more. Taste; you may want to add another splash of fish sauce or lime juice. Serve garnished with the cilantro, or store in an airtight container in the refrigerator for up to 5 days or in the freezer for up to 3 months.

julie's hungarian sweet-and-sour cabbage soup

makes 6 servings | prep time: 15 minutes | cook time: 45 minutes

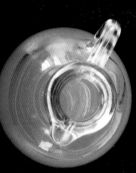

Here's a big shout-out to my soup sister, Julie Burford, for creating an insanely good brew. Cabbage soups have been a staple of Eastern European cooking since way back when, and if you're in my age bracket, you remember cabbage soup diets being all the rage back in the seventies and eighties. I'm not saying you should have this soup seven days in a row (though you could), but even one hit is enough to supercharge your system. Cabbage is a top detoxifying cruciferous vegetable, and Julie has really amped up the taste by creating a sweet-and-sour profile with coconut palm sugar (or maple syrup) playing off apple cider vinegar. Wow!

1 pound red cabbage, quartered

2 tablespoons extra-virgin olive oil

1 yellow onion, finely diced

Sea salt

1 unpeeled crisp red apple, coarsely grated

1 teaspoon caraway seeds

Freshly ground black pepper

2 tablespoons apple cider vinegar

1 tablespoon coconut palm sugar or dark maple syrup

6 cups Magic Mineral Broth (page 35), Pastured Beef Bone Broth (page 43), or Nourishing Bone Broth (page 41)

2 tablespoons full-fat plain yogurt, for garnish

Shred the cabbage in a food processor or slice it thinly with a knife.

Heat the olive oil in a soup pot over medium heat, then add the onion and a pinch of salt and sauté until translucent, about 6 minutes. Add the cabbage and ¼ teaspoon salt and sauté for another 5 minutes. Add the apple, caraway seeds, ½ teaspoon black pepper, and ¼ teaspoon salt and sauté for 1 minute more. Add the vinegar, sugar, and ½ cup of broth to deglaze the pot, stirring to loosen any bits stuck to the bottom, and cook until the liquid is reduced by half.

Add the remaining 5½ cups of broth, decrease the heat to low, cover, and simmer for 30 to 35 minutes, or until tender. Taste; you may want to add a pinch of salt or a few grinds of pepper. To serve, ladle the soup into bowls and garnish each with a teaspoon of yogurt or store in an airtight container in the refrigerator for up to 5 days or in the freezer for up to 3 months.

very gingery and garlicky chicken soup

makes 6 servings | prep time: 20 minutes | cook time: 30 minutes

Sometimes I feel more like a mad scientist than a cook. That's what soup-making and a pantry full of ingredients can do to you. I've noted that soups lend themselves to experimentation because they're such a forgiving milieu, and here I've created a hybrid of chicken soup and miso soup. Miso has that elusive taste known as umami (pronounced "OOH-mommy"), which lends heft to the brew. The miso matches well with the garlic, ginger, and shiitake mushrooms (another source of umami). And because the miso goes in at the end, when the soup is already hot, its probiotics are preserved. That's great news for your digestion.

2 tablespoons extra-virgin olive oil

1 yellow onion, finely diced

6 fresh shiitake mushrooms, stemmed and sliced

2 carrots, peeled and finely diced

4 stalks celery, finely chopped

Sea salt

4 cloves garlic, minced

1 tablespoon finely chopped fresh ginger

2 teaspoons freshly grated turmeric, or ½ teaspoon ground turmeric

6 cups Old-Fashioned Chicken Stock (page 39) or Magic Mineral Broth (page 35)

1½ cups cooked and cubed organic chicken breast (see Cook's Note on page 92)

1 tablespoon white miso

2 teaspoons freshly squeezed lemon juice

2 scallions, white and green parts, sliced diagonally

2 cups loosely packed watercress or baby spinach

Heat the olive oil in a soup pot over medium heat, then add the onion, mushrooms, carrots, celery, and ¼ teaspoon salt and sauté just until golden, about 8 minutes. Stir in the garlic, ginger, and turmeric and cook for another minute. Pour in ½ cup of the stock to deglaze the pot, stirring to loosen any bits stuck to the bottom, and cook until the liquid is reduced by half.

Add the remaining 5½ cups of stock, bring to a boil over medium heat, then decrease the heat to low, cover, and simmer for 20 minutes. Add the chicken. Ladle ¼ cup of the hot broth into a small bowl, add the miso, and stir with a fork until the miso is dissolved. Stir the mixture back into the soup. Stir in the lemon juice and scallions. To serve, distribute the watercress among six bowls and ladle in the soup. Or store in an airtight container in the refrigerator for up to 5 days or in the freezer for up to 3 months.

provençal lentil soup

makes 6 servings | prep time: 15 minutes | cook time: 35 minutes

This soup proves that French fare can be light and not laden with cream. Herbes de Provence is a mixture of herbs traditionally gathered from the southeastern French countryside. It includes marjoram, rosemary, oregano, and thyme, with lavender sometimes thrown in. To me, thyme is the noteworthy ingredient; when dried it retains its flavor better than many herbs, and its oils are renowned for having antimicrobial and antibacterial properties. Another nutritional superstar in this recipe is the lentils, whose high fiber content is great for stabilizing blood sugar. Lentils also create a hearty mouth sensation, leaving you feeling as though you've just eaten a nice, satiating meal.

2 tablespoons extra-virgin olive oil

1 yellow onion, diced small

Sea salt

2 carrots, peeled and diced small

2 stalks celery, diced small

2 cloves garlic, minced

1½ teaspoons herbes de Provence (see Cook's Note)

¼ teaspoon freshly ground black pepper

1 (14.5-ounce) can diced tomatoes, drained

1 cup dried French green lentils, rinsed well

6 cups Magic Mineral Broth (page 35)

1 bay leaf

Freshly squeezed lemon juice (optional)

3 cups tightly packed baby spinach

2 tablespoons Many Herb Drizzle (page 127), for garnish

cook's note: If you don't have herbes de Provence in your spice cabinet, substitute ½ teaspoon dried thyme, ¼ teaspoon dried oregano, ¼ teaspoon dried rosemary, and ½ teaspoon ground fennel seed.

Heat the olive oil in a soup pot over medium heat, then add the onion and a pinch of salt and sauté until translucent, about 4 minutes. Add the carrots, celery, and ½ teaspoon salt and sauté until all of the vegetables are tender and turning golden brown, about 8 minutes. Add the garlic and sauté for about 30 seconds, then stir in the herbes de Provence, pepper, and ¼ teaspoon salt.

Stir in the tomatoes and lentils, then add the broth and bay leaf. Increase the heat to high and bring to a boil. Decrease the heat to low, cover, and simmer until the lentils are tender, about 25 minutes. Taste; you may want to add a spritz of lemon juice or up to ½ teaspoon salt. To serve, divide the spinach among six bowls, ladle the soup over the spinach, and top with the drizzle. Or store in an airtight container in the refrigerator for up to 5 days or in the freezer for up to 3 months.

simplest chicken pho

makes 6 servings | prep time: 15 minutes | cook time: 25 minutes

The traditional Vietnamese soup pho (pronounced "fuh") is a mixture of Chinese and French cuisines. Pho can take a long time to cook, but I've come up with a shortcut. Here you take out your cheesecloth, put in spices including coriander seeds and peppercorns, and add cut-up ginger and onion. Then you tie the cheesecloth like a hobo sack to the corner of the pot and delight as the aromatics infuse into the pot. In 20 minutes you have pho broth, into which you place the rice noodles. Finish the pho with a garnish of thinly sliced jalapeños, mung bean sprouts, Thai basil, and mint, and you've got an incredibly nourishing dish that's exploding with flavor.

broth

1 (4-inch) piece fresh ginger, unpeeled and sliced

2 teaspoons coriander seeds, toasted in a dry skillet for about 30 seconds, until fragrant

2 whole cloves

1 teaspoon black peppercorns

1 small yellow onion, halved

2 quarts Old-Fashioned Chicken Stock (page 39)

1 teaspoon sea salt

1 tablespoon plus 1 teaspoon coconut palm sugar

1 tablespoon plus 2 teaspoons fish sauce, plus more if needed

bowls

1 pound thin rice noodles (see Variation)

1½ cups cooked and shredded organic chicken (see Cook's Note on page 92)

4 scallions, green part only, thinly sliced

¼ cup chopped fresh cilantro

garnishes

2 cups mung bean sprouts

12 sprigs fresh mint

12 sprigs fresh Thai basil

1 jalapeño pepper, seeded and thinly sliced

2 limes, cut into wedges

Wrap the ginger, coriander seeds, cloves, peppercorns, and onion in an 11 by 16-inch piece of cheesecloth. Tie the cheesecloth with butcher's twine, leaving a few extra inches to secure the pouch to the pot. In a soup pot, combine the stock, salt, sugar, and fish sauce. Secure the herb pouch to the soup pot, making sure it's completely submerged in the stock, and bring it to a boil over medium-high heat. Decrease the heat to medium-low, cover, and simmer for 20 minutes. Remove and discard the spice bag. Taste; you may want to add a bit more fish sauce.

Meanwhile, in a large bowl, soak the rice noodles in warm water until softened, about 10 minutes. Bring a large saucepan of salted water to a boil, add the noodles, and cook for 3 minutes, or just until tender. Drain well.

To assemble, divide the noodles and chicken among 6 bowls, ladle in broth to cover, and top with the scallions and cilantro. Serve with a plate of the bean sprouts, mint, basil, jalapeño, and lime wedges alongside. Or store in an airtight container in the refrigerator for up to 5 days or in the freezer for up to 3 months.

cook's note: Play with the timing on the noodles. If you cook them until al dente, they will finish cooking in the hot broth.

variation: If you don't want to use rice noodles, try spiralized zucchini or daikon noodles instead.

clean-out-the-fridge soup

makes 6 servings | prep time: 15 minutes | cook time: 40 minutes

I came up with this soup by polling my friends and neighbors to see what they had sitting in their fridges. The whole point is that veggies no longer in their prime are still perfect for a hearty vegetable soup. Here the culinary color wheel came up with orange (carrots and sweet potato), tan (parsnip), and green (kale, although you could use chard or spinach). Throw in a can of tomatoes and a tablespoon of tomato paste from the pantry, along with some quinoa and spices, and you have a scrumptious soup.

3 tablespoons extra-virgin olive oil

1 yellow onion, diced

Sea salt

2 carrots, peeled and diced

2 stalks celery, diced

2 parsnips, peeled and diced

1 sweet potato, peeled and cut into ¼-inch cubes

2 cloves garlic, minced

½ teaspoon dried thyme

½ teaspoon dried oregano

⅛ teaspoon red pepper flakes

6 cups Magic Mineral Broth (page 35), Pastured Beef Bone Broth (page 43), or Nourishing Bone Broth (page 41)

1 tablespoon tomato paste

1 (14.5-ounce) can diced tomatoes

1 bay leaf

1 cup cooked quinoa

1 small bunch kale, Swiss chard, or spinach, chopped into bite-size pieces

Heat the olive oil in a soup pot over medium heat, then add the onion and a pinch of salt and sauté until translucent, about 4 minutes. Add the carrots, celery, parsnips, sweet potato, and ¼ teaspoon salt and sauté until all of the vegetables are tender and turning deep golden brown, about 12 minutes. Add the garlic and sauté for about 30 seconds, then stir in the thyme, oregano, red pepper flakes, and ½ teaspoon salt. Pour in ½ cup of the broth to deglaze the pot, stirring to loosen any bits stuck to the bottom, and cook until the liquid is reduced by half.

Stir in the tomato paste, tomatoes, bay leaf, and the remaining 5½ cups of broth. Increase the heat to high and bring to a boil. Decrease the heat to low, cover, and simmer until the vegetables are tender, about 15 minutes. Stir in the quinoa and kale and cook for 3 minutes, or until the kale is just tender. Taste; you may want to add another generous pinch of salt. Store in an airtight container in the refrigerator for up to 5 days or in the freezer for up to 3 months.

triple mushroom soup

makes 6 servings | prep time: 20 minutes | cook time: 35 minutes

This is my shout-out to umami (pronounced "OOH-mommy"). Umami is that hard-to-explain rich, savory taste that certain foods produce. Here, there's umami everywhere you look. The mushrooms, tomato paste, and tamari are full of umami. So is the bone broth. Hearty doesn't even begin to describe this soup, which is rounded out with onion, black pepper, parsley, thyme, and a tiny hit of lemon juice. This is one of those soups where you dive in and don't come up for air until you're done.

2 tablespoons extra-virgin olive oil

1 yellow onion, diced small

1 pound crimini mushrooms, stemmed and coarsely chopped (see Cook's Note)

4 ounces shiitake mushrooms, stemmed and coarsely chopped

4 ounces oyster mushrooms, stemmed and coarsely chopped

Sea salt

2 stalks celery, diced

1 carrot, diced

¼ teaspoon freshly ground black pepper

2 cloves garlic, minced

2 teaspoons fresh thyme, or ½ teaspoon dried thyme

2 tablespoons tamari

1½ tablespoons tomato paste

6 cups Nourishing Bone Broth (page 41) or Pastured Beef Bone Broth (page 43)

1 teaspoon freshly squeezed lemon juice, plus more if needed

2 tablespoons chopped fresh flat-leaf parsley, for garnish

Heat the olive oil in a soup pot over medium heat, then add the onion, mushrooms, and a pinch of salt and sauté until golden brown and caramelized, about 20 minutes. Add the celery, carrot, pepper, and ½ teaspoon salt and sauté for another 6 minutes. Stir in the garlic and thyme and cook until fragrant, about 1 minute. Stir in the tamari, tomato paste, and ½ cup of the broth to deglaze the pot, stirring to loosen any bits stuck to the bottom, and cook until the liquid is reduced by half.

Add the remaining 5½ cups of broth and ¼ teaspoon salt. Bring to a boil over medium heat, then stir in the lemon juice. Taste; you may want to add another generous pinch of salt or a bit more lemon juice. Serve garnished with the parsley, or store in an airtight container in the refrigerator for up to 5 days or in the freezer for up to 3 months.

cook's note: To shorten your prep time, place all of the mushrooms in a food processor and pulse a few times until coarsely chopped. Don't over-process or you'll end up with mushroom mush.

mini meatballs in broth

makes 6 servings | prep time: 15 minutes | cook time: 15 minutes

A simple bowl of broth hosts these mini meatballs, which are closer to the Latin-American version known as *albondigas*. The meatball mixture comes together quickly, and the best part—no rolling! All you need is a melon baller or a tablespoon. They're so small and delicate the hot broth will cook them in minutes. Sometimes it's the simplest soups that grab our imaginations and our taste buds. These meatballs are also lovely in Very Gingery Garlicky Chicken Soup (page 106), Clean-Out-the-Fridge Soup (page 110), Nana's Chicken Soup with Zucchini Noodles (page 96), Herby Tuscan Bean and Vegetable Soup (page 94) and Latin American Chicken Soup with Greens (page 92).

1 organic egg, beaten

⅓ cup cooked basmati or jasmine rice

¼ cup finely chopped fresh parsley or basil

1 tablespoon chopped fresh thyme, or 1 teaspoon dried

1 tablespoon chopped fresh oregano, or 1 teaspoon dried

2 teaspoons minced garlic

1 teaspoon crushed fennel seeds

½ teaspoon sea salt

¼ teaspoon red pepper flakes

1 pound organic ground dark-meat chicken or turkey

8 cups Old-Fashioned Chicken Stock (page 39), Chicken Magic Mineral Broth (page 38), or Magic Mineral Broth (page 35)

2 tablespoons finely chopped parsley (garnish)

To make the meatballs place the egg, rice, parsley, thyme, oregano, garlic, fennel seeds, salt, and red pepper flakes in a bowl and stir to combine. Add the chicken, and mix with your hands or a spatula until just combined (see Cook's Note).

In a soup pot, heat the broth over medium-high heat. When the broth reaches a slow boil, use a melon baller or tablespoon to scoop out balls of the chicken mixture and gently lower them into the pot. Cover and simmer for 10 minutes, or until the meatballs are cooked all the way through. Serve garnished with the parsley, or store in an airtight container in the refrigerator for up to 5 days or in the freezer for up to 3 months.

variation: For a change of flavor, swap out the thyme, oregano, and fennel for a tablespoon of freshly grated ginger.

cook's note: When it comes to making meatballs, it's best to use a gentle touch. In this recipe, all the other ingredients are first mixed together in a bowl. That way, all you have to do is lightly work in the meat and—voilà!—you'll have meatballs that cook up light and fluffy.

cauliflower korma soup

makes 6 servings | prep time: 15 minutes | cook time: 30 minutes

This is my riff on korma, a traditional Turkish and Persian side dish. *Korma* means "to braise," and cauliflower is the ideal braising vegetable. It stands up to the simmering liquid, soaking in all the aromatics without breaking apart. Normally kormas are thick and creamy, but here I've forgone the cream without losing any of the irresistible signature spiciness. Kormas demand coriander and cumin, and here I've doubled up on the cumin, using both the seeds and the ground version. Kormas can be mild or fiery. This is a one-alarmer.

2 tablespoons extra-virgin olive oil

1 yellow onion, diced small

Sea salt

1 tablespoon minced fresh ginger

2 cloves garlic, minced

1 teaspoon cumin seeds

1 (2-pound) head cauliflower, chopped into bite-size florets

1 sweet potato, peeled and diced

1 teaspoon ground coriander

½ heaping teaspoon ground turmeric

½ teaspoon ground cumin

¼ teaspoon freshly ground black pepper

⅛ teaspoon red pepper flakes

1 (14.5-ounce) can diced tomatoes, drained and juice reserved

6 cups Magic Mineral Broth (page 35)

½ teaspoon freshly squeezed lemon juice

2 tablespoons chopped fresh cilantro, for garnish

Heat the olive oil in a soup pot over medium heat, then add the onion and a pinch of salt and cook until translucent and slightly golden, about 6 minutes. Stir in the ginger, garlic, and cumin seeds and cook for another 30 seconds. Add the cauliflower, sweet potato, coriander, turmeric, ground cumin, black pepper, red pepper flakes, and ½ teaspoon salt, stirring until coated. Add the reserved tomato juice and ½ cup of the broth to deglaze the pot, stirring to loosen any bits stuck to the bottom, and cook until the liquid is reduced by half.

Add the remaining 5½ cups of broth and bring to a boil. Decrease the heat to medium-low and simmer until the vegetables are tender, about 20 minutes. Stir in the lemon juice and ½ teaspoon salt. Serve garnished with the cilantro, or store in an airtight container in the refrigerator for up to 5 days or in the freezer for up to 3 months.

mediterranean fish soup

makes 4 servings | prep time: 15 minutes | cook time: 20 minutes

If you want to emulate a group of long-lived people, look no further than those who subsist on a Mediterranean diet. Here's a staple of that diet: a simple yet hearty fish soup. It's easy because all you do is poach the fish in the aromatic broth for 4 minutes, and it's ready to go. Any white fish will do, be it halibut, black cod, or bass. The fish pairs with shrimp and provides a blast of protein and energizing vitamin B_{12}. Poaching keeps the fish nice and moist, and the herb drizzle is a delicious finishing touch.

2 teaspoons extra-virgin olive oil

1 onion, diced

1 fennel bulb, diced

Sea salt

2 cloves garlic, minced

⅛ teaspoon red pepper flakes

1 (14½-ounce) can diced tomatoes

3 cups Magic Mineral Broth (page 35) or Old-Fashioned Chicken Stock (page 39)

1 pound white-fleshed fish, such as halibut, black cod, or bass, cut into 2-inch pieces

1 pound large shrimp, peeled and deveined

1 teaspoon lemon zest

¼ teaspoon freshly ground black pepper

1 tablespoon chopped fresh parsley

¼ cup Many Herb Drizzle (page 127; optional), for garnish

Heat the olive oil in a soup pot over medium-high heat, then add the onion, fennel, and ¼ teaspoon salt and sauté until the vegetables begin to soften, 3 to 5 minutes. Stir in the garlic and red pepper flakes and sauté for 30 seconds more. Stir in the tomatoes with their juice and ¼ teaspoon salt to deglaze the pot, stirring to loosen any bits stuck to the bottom.

Add the broth and bring to a boil. Decrease the heat to low, cover, and simmer until the vegetables are just tender, about 8 minutes. Gently stir in the fish and shrimp and simmer until the seafood is tender and cooked through (it should be just opaque), about 4 minutes. Stir in the lemon zest, black pepper, and parsley. Taste; you may want to add a pinch or two of salt. Serve garnished with the herb drizzle, or store in an airtight container in the refrigerator for up to 3 days or in the freezer for up to 3 months.

soup toppers

The surest way to make someone think you've upped your culinary game is to create toppers for soups. I think toppers are the key to building what I call "culinary muscle memory." The nine toppers below (with a few variations thrown in) can be mixed and matched with soups throughout the book. Once you know the taste and texture preferences of those you're cooking for, don't be surprised if you find yourself experimenting with these toppers. It's like accessorizing an outfit or, as my friend describes it, putting edible makeup on a soup. Nut creams, crumbles, gremolatas, drizzles, salsas—you'll find them all here, waiting to adorn your next bowl of yum.

my favorite combinations

topper	soup
Chermoula (page 122)	Moroccan Carrot Soup (page 51)
	Greek Cucumber Yogurt Soup (page 52)
Crispy Shiitake Mushrooms (page 123)	Celeriac Soup with Crispy Shiitake Mushrooms (page 79)
Crunchy Kale Crumbles (page 125)	Power Green Soup (page 58)
	Gingery Broccoli Soup with Mint (page 60)
	Spiced Butternut Squash Soup with Cardamom and Ginger (page 78)
Many Herb Drizzle (page 127)	Avocado Citrus Soup (page 48)
	Greek Cucumber Yogurt Soup (page 52)
	Silk Road Pumpkin Soup (page 57)
	Gingery Broccoli Soup with Mint (page 60)
	Sweet Pea and Mint Soup (page 71)
	Summer Zucchini Soup with Basil (page 73)
	Roasted Heirloom Tomato Soup (page 75)
	Escarole Soup (page 77)
	Celeriac Soup with Crispy Shiitake Mushrooms (page 79)
	Provençal Lentil Soup (page 107)
	Mediterranean Fish Soup (page 116)

topper	soup
Kale Gremolata (page 128)	Power Green Soup (page 58)
	Gingery Broccoli Soup with Mint (page 60)
	Spiced Butternut Squash Soup with Cardamom and Ginger (page 78)
Silken Nut Cream (page 129)	Roasted Apple and Butternut Squash Soup (page 47)
	Springtime Asparagus and Leek Soup (page 49)
	Power Green Soup (page 58)
	Gingery Broccoli Soup with Mint (page 60)
	Spiced Butternut Squash Soup with Cardamom and Ginger (page 78)
	Celeriac Soup with Crispy Shiitake Mushrooms (page 79)
Fresh Soup Salsas (pages 132 and 133)	Avocado Citrus Soup (page 48)
	Greek Cucumber Yogurt Soup (page 52)
	Not Your Average Gazpacho (page 53)
	Power Green Soup (page 58)
	Gingery Broccoli Soup with Mint (page 60)
	Summer Zucchini Soup with Basil (page 73)
	Roasted Heirloom Tomato Soup (page 75)
	Escarole Soup (page 77)
Parsnip Chips (page 134)	Moroccan Carrot Soup (page 51)
	Silk Road Pumpkin Soup (page 57)
	Spiced Butternut Squash Soup with Cardamom and Ginger (page 78)
Polenta Croutons (page 137)	Cuban Black Bean Soup (page 87)
	Latin American Chicken Soup with Greens (page 92)
	Smoky Split Pea Soup (page 99)

chermoula

makes 1¼ cups | prep time: 5 minutes | cook time: none

Normally, Moroccan chermoulas are used as a marinade with meat or fish. But a little tinkering yields an extraordinary drizzle that works mighty fine on top of a soup. Mint, parsley, cumin, paprika, olive oil, and lemon juice all combine to create a chermoula with some serious zing!

1 cup tightly packed chopped fresh flat-leaf parsley

½ cup tightly packed fresh cilantro or basil leaves

6 fresh mint leaves

½ teaspoon ground cumin

½ teaspoon paprika

1 clove garlic, chopped

¼ cup extra-virgin olive oil

3 tablespoons freshly squeezed lemon juice

¼ teaspoon sea salt

Combine all of the ingredients in a food processor and process until well blended. Store in an airtight container in the refrigerator for up to 5 days or in the freezer for up to 3 months.

crispy shiitake mushrooms

makes 1 cup | prep time: 5 minutes | cook time: 20 minutes

I swear people mistake these for bacon all the time, which isn't really as strange as it sounds. Mushrooms are loaded with savory umami taste, as is bacon, and baking shiitakes leaves them crispy, just like you-know-what. The smell of the shiitakes baking is absolutely intoxicating. Make sure that they're lined up single-file on the baking sheet and not piled on top of each other, otherwise they'll steam instead of bake.

1 pound fresh shiitake mushrooms, stemmed and thinly sliced

2 tablespoons extra-virgin olive oil

¼ teaspoon sea salt

¼ teaspoon smoked paprika

Preheat the oven to 375°F. Line a baking sheet with parchment paper.

Place the shiitakes in a bowl, drizzle with the olive oil, and sprinkle with the salt and paprika, then toss until evenly coated. Arrange the mushrooms in a single layer on the prepared baking sheet and roast until crisp and browned, about 20 minutes. Store in an airtight container at room temperature for up to 2 days.

crunchy kale crumbles

makes 6 cups | prep time: 5 minutes | cook time: 10 minutes

This recipe is incredibly easy to make: just some torn-up kale coated with olive oil and salt that gets popped into the oven. The alchemy of the cooking takes away the kale's bitterness, leaving you with an irresistible garnish that's perfect atop a bowl of soup.

1 large bunch kale, stemmed and torn into 2-inch pieces

1 tablespoon extra-virgin olive oil

½ teaspoon sea salt

Preheat the oven to 300°F. Line a rimmed baking sheet with parchment paper.

Put all of the ingredients in a large bowl and toss until the kale is well coated. Spread the kale on the prepared baking sheet in a single layer. Bake for 10 minutes, or until nice and crisp. (If it isn't crisp after 10 minutes, bake in 5-minute increments until it crisps up.) Remove from the oven and let cool for 5 minutes. Crumble the crispy kale into small pieces and store in an airtight container at room temperature for up to 5 days.

many herb drizzle

makes ½ cup | prep time: 5 minutes | cook time: none

Drizzles are designed to brighten up everything they touch, and they can be found in nearly every culture's cooking. France? It's a *pistou*. Italy? Pesto. Morocco? *Chermoula*. They're all made similarly: herbs, olive oil, lemon juice, and salt go into a food processor, and what comes out is a fine dining refinement, if you will, for everyday soup.

1 cup tightly packed chopped fresh flat-leaf parsley

½ cup tightly packed fresh mint leaves

2 tablespoons chopped fresh chives

2 tablespoons freshly squeezed lemon juice

¼ teaspoon sea salt

¼ cup extra-virgin olive oil

Combine all of the ingredients in a food processor and process until well blended. For a thinner drizzle, add 1 tablespoon of water. Store in an airtight container in the refrigerator for up to 5 days.

variation: For an infusion of Asian or Latino flavor, substitute cilantro for the parsley.

kale gremolata

makes ¾ cup | prep time: 5 minutes | cook time: none

Here I am, getting all fancy again. Gremolatas are garnishes—usually made of chopped parsley, grated lemon zest, and garlic. Me being me, I just have to tinker with things, so sometimes I swap cilantro for parsley and orange zest for lemon zest and, what the heck, throw some basil into the mix. Don't worry: it works.

1 small bunch kale, stemmed and finely chopped

⅓ cup finely chopped fresh flat-leaf parsley

1 tablespoon finely chopped fresh mint

Grated zest of 1 lemon

1 clove garlic, minced

Put all of the ingredients in a small bowl and stir to combine. Store in an airtight container in the refrigerator for up to 2 days.

silken nut cream

makes 2 cups | prep time: 5 minutes | cook time: none

I've been making and using nut creams since I first realized that they offer all the richness of butter but have a far better nutritional profile. They give an incredible mouthfeel to soup; it's like a luscious hit of yum that you're not expecting. I play with cashew, almond, pistachio, and walnut creams, as each has a slightly different taste.

1 cup raw nuts, such as cashews, pistachios, walnuts (see Cook's Note), or almonds

1 cup water

1 teaspoon freshly squeezed lemon juice

¼ teaspoon sea salt

Put all of the ingredients in a food processor and process until creamy smooth, about 1 minute. Store in an airtight container in the refrigerator for up to 7 days or in the freezer for up to 3 months.

variation: For an herbaceous note, add ½ cup chopped fresh basil or mint.

cook's note: If using walnuts, add ¼ teaspoon of maple syrup to counteract any bitterness that might come from the skins.

fresh soup salsas

Salsa, whether you're talking dance or food, is a mix of styles that when you put them together is, frankly, hot. Typically, salsa fresca is made from tomatoes, onions, jalapeños, lime juice, and salt. But salsa was made for improvisation; sometimes I forego tomato and make radish the star—or avocado. As a sauce (and *salsa* is Spanish for "sauce"), salsa just makes me want to riff. It will have the same effect on you.

heirloom tomato salsa

makes 2 cups | prep time: 10 minutes | cook time: none

1½ cups finely diced fresh heirloom or Roma tomatoes

¼ cup finely diced red onion

2 tablespoons chopped fresh flat-leaf parsley or basil

2 teaspoons freshly squeezed lemon juice

2 tablespoons extra-virgin olive oil

Pinch of red pepper flakes

¼ teaspoon sea salt

In a medium bowl, combine all of the ingredients. Cover and refrigerate until ready to use, or for up to 3 days.

avocado and cucumber salsa

makes 3 cups | prep time: 10 minutes | cook time: none

1 cucumber, diced

1 avocado, diced

1 small red bell pepper, finely diced

3 tablespoons finely chopped fresh cilantro or flat-leaf parsley

2 tablespoons freshly squeezed lime juice

1 tablespoon extra-virgin olive oil

¼ teaspoon sea salt

Pinch of cayenne pepper

In a medium bowl, combine all of the ingredients. Cover and refrigerate until ready to use, or for up to 3 days.

fresh radish, fennel, and herb salsa

makes 2 cups | prep time: 10 minutes | cook time: none

12 radishes, coarsely chopped

1 fennel bulb, finely chopped

3 tablespoons chopped fresh
flat-leaf parsley

1 tablespoon chopped fresh mint

2 tablespoons extra-virgin
olive oil

1½ tablespoons freshly squeezed
lemon juice

¼ teaspoon sea salt

¼ teaspoon freshly ground black
pepper

In a medium bowl, combine all of the ingredients. Cover and refrigerate until ready to use, or for up to 3 days.

parsnip chips

makes 2 cups | prep time: 15 minutes | cook time: 25 minutes

Sometimes you just want some crunch on top of your soup, and, boy, do these parsnip chips deliver. I use a mandoline to slice the chips paper-thin, then give them a quick coating of olive oil, salt, and curry powder. Into the oven they go, and then comes the hard part: letting them cook slowly. I'm talking 300°F instead of 450°F, which is the difference between getting a perfect chip versus one that's charbroiled.

These chips are like cookies: let them cool for a few minutes and you won't believe how crunchy and yummy they become. Place them on top of the Silk Road Pumpkin Soup (page 57) for a truly transcendent taste.

2 parsnips, thinly sliced

1 tablespoon extra-virgin olive oil

½ teaspoon sea salt

½ teaspoon curry powder

Preheat the oven to 300°F. Line a rimmed baking sheet with parchment paper.

Put all of the ingredients in a bowl and toss until well combined. Arrange the parsnips on the prepared baking sheet in a single layer, making sure they don't overlap, and bake for 25 minutes, or until golden brown and crispy. Check the chips at 20 minutes to prevent burning. Allow to cool completely on the baking sheet. Store in an airtight container at room temperature for up to 3 days.

variation: Replace the curry powder with your favorite spice to suit your taste buds.

polenta croutons

makes 2 cups | prep time: 10 minutes | cook time: 25 minutes

Bread croutons are so yesterday, but these are a fantastic update, especially if you can't eat gluten and are normally crouton-deprived. In the old days, I used to stand by the stove stirring polenta forever. Now it's so much easier, as precooked polenta logs are available in just about any supermarket. Cube 'em; add olive oil, salt, and spices; and toss—then bake. In 25 minutes you have croutons. Best of all, you can make a lot because they freeze and reheat well.

9 ounces or ½ log precooked polenta, cut into ½-inch cubes (see Cook's Note)

2 teaspoons extra-virgin olive oil

1 teaspoon sea salt

½ teaspoon freshly ground pepper

Fresh herbs, such as parsley, thyme, or rosemary (optional), finely chopped

Preheat the oven to 400°F. Line a rimmed baking sheet with parchment paper.

In a bowl, toss all of the ingredients together until the polenta is well coated. Spread the polenta cubes on the prepared baking sheet, making sure they aren't touching. Bake for 25 minutes, or until golden brown and crisp on the outside. Store in an airtight container in the refrigerator for up to 3 days or in the freezer for up to 1 month.

cook's note: Precooked polenta logs can be found in most grocery stores. I like Trader Joe's organic polenta and Food Merchants organic traditional polenta.

resource guide

Where can you find everything from a big, sixteen-quart stockpot to kombu to information on local farmers' markets? The Internet, of course. Here's a list of websites you might find useful in procuring tools and ingredients to make you a soup master.

SOUP POTS AND STOCKPOTS

William Sonoma
williams-sonoma.com

Sur la Table
surlatable.com

Bed Bath and Beyond
bedbathandbeyond.com

Le Creuset
lecreuset.com

Amazon
amazon.com

SLOW COOKERS

All Clad
all-clad.com

ELECTRIC PRESSURE COOKERS

Instant Pot
instantpot.com

BLENDERS

Vitamix
vitamix.com

STORAGE

Ball Jars (freezer safe)
freshpreserving.com

Weck Jars
weckjars.com

Snapware
snapware.com

PANTRY INGREDIENTS

Organic coconut palm sugar
bigtreefarms.com

Sea salt
selinanaturally.com

Kombu
seaveg.com

Maple syrup
maplevalleysyrup.coop

Healthy cooking oils
spectrumorganics.com

Grass-fed and humanely raised
beef and chicken
grasslandbeef.com

Sustainable seafood and
grass-fed beef
vitalchoice.com

SPICES

Spicely
spicely.com

Whole Spice
wholespice.com

ONLINE MARKETS

Local Harvest
localharvest.org

Organic Provisions
orgfood.com

Sun Organic Farms
sunorganic.com

GROCERY CHAINS WITH WELL-STOCKED ORGANIC PRODUCTS

Safeway
safeway.com

Sprouts Farmers Markets
sprouts.com

Trader Joe's
traderjoes.com

Whole Foods
wholefoodsmarket.com

FARMERS' MARKETS AND LOCAL FOODS

Eat Well Guide (directory to local,
sustainable, and organic farmers'
markets, restaurants, stores, bakeries,
and more)
eatwellguide.org

acknowledgments

The aroma of soup simmering on the stove created the backdrop for a wonderful community to lend their creative talents to making this book possible.

My thanks to the following:

The Grande Dame of soup-making, my mother, Barbara P. Katz, whose love went into every drop she's ever made, and my late father, Jay Katz, who never met a bowl of soup he didn't devour with gusto. My soup sister and dearest friend, Julie F. Buford, who has stood by the stove with me making soup for more than 10 years; her husband, Stan, a super soup eater; Josie, the wonder dog who licked the spoons; and granddaughter Julia Isaac, who stood by the stove with me and helped with the creations inside this book.

Tremendous thanks to my co-author Mat Edelson. This is our fifth book together, and I wonder if he ever thought he would be a soup whisperer? No matter the subject matter, his wit and words make every story that much better. A special shout-out to the extraordinary Deb Cohen for loaning out Mat for yet another project and being so supportive of our work.

Jeremy Katz, wonderful agent, friend, and advocate who knows a good soup when he tastes one.

The talented people at Ten Speed Press: publisher Aaron Wehner and editorial director Julie Bennett, for their belief in this book; Kelly Snowden, my editor who thought of me for this dream project and delivered absolutely pitch perfect editorial direction; Kara Plikaitis, for her keen creative eye, amazing art direction, and splendid design of these beautiful pages; and Emma Campion, the wonderful creative director at Ten Speed.

Thanks to Amanda Poulsen Dix, for your copyediting prowess; Jasmine Star, for proofreading the text; Hannah Rahill, Michele Crim, and Ashley Matuzak, for their sales and marketing expertise; and Daniel Wilkey, for his public relations and social media savvy. For the stunning photography, I bow in gratitude to photographer Eva Kolenko and her assistant Soraya Matos; Claire Mack, prop stylist extraordinaire; and the brilliant food stylist Jeffrey Larsen; and the delightful Amy Hatwig.

None of my books would be as fun to work on without the collaboration of my dear friend and colleague, Catherine McConkie, who is simply the most creative culinary wizard I know. Thanks to Jessica Paulson, who kept me in broth and tested many of the recipes, and my loyal canine assistants, Lola and her new sidekick Blossom.

Many thanks to my partners at Healing Kitchens; Jen Yasis, my "Jen-eral" in all things; Paul Remer, who keeps me on my toes at all times; and to all my friends and colleagues at Commonweal. Also, Jo Cooper, dear friend, colleague, and my marketing impresario. You continue to be a valued treasure!

A big thank you to my family; Jeff, Jill, Harry, Amelia, Andy, Asako, Branden, and my husband Gregg Kellogg, for always supporting my work no matter what, and for giving me a wonderful reason to make soup.

And lastly, a culinary hug and a big thank you to all of my cheerleaders, friends, colleagues, and readers for years of inspiration.

about the authors

Rebecca Katz is an accomplished chef and national speaker who has worked with the country's top wellness leaders. She is the author of the award-winning *The Cancer-Fighting Kitchen*, *The Longevity Kitchen*, and *The Healthy Mind Cookbook*, as well as the founder of *Healing Kitchens*. She lives in the San Francisco Bay Area with her husband and two loyal kitchen dogs, Lola and Blossom, making soup. Visit RebeccaKatz.com for more information.

Mat Edelson is an award-winning science, health, and sports writer. He is the former anchor/director of the Johns Hopkins Health Newsfeed, a nationally syndicated daily radio program. This is the fifth book he has co-authored with Rebecca Katz. He lives in Washington, DC.

Photo credit Jeffrey G. Katz

Photo credit Doug McDonough

index

Published in the United States by Ten Speed Press,
an imprint of the Crown Publishing Group, a division of
Penguin Random House LLC, New York.
www.crownpublishing.com
www.tenspeed.com

Ten Speed Press and the Ten Speed Press
colophon are registered trademarks of
Penguin Random House LLC.

Library of Congress Cataloging-in-Publication Data
is on file with the publisher.

Hardcover ISBN: 978-0-399-57825-0
eBook ISBN: 978-0-399-57826-7

Printed in China

Design by Kara Plikaitis

10 9 8 7 6 5 4 3 2 1

First Edition